CHROMATIC DREAMS

This book was created to offer a one-of-a-kind coloring experience that stands out from the thousands of others on the market. It's an experiment of sorts, born from a desire to create something truly exceptional. I have noticed that a lot of adult coloring books still retain a childlike appearance, and this is my attempt to break free from that mold.

While coloring these intricate illustrations may prove more challenging than other coloring books, that's the beauty of it. You'll feel a great sense of pride and accomplishment once you've completed each page. Don't worry though, there's a guide-illustration to help you along the way — but feel free to deviate from the suggested color palette and let your imagination run wild. This book is your canvas, so create your own unique masterpiece.

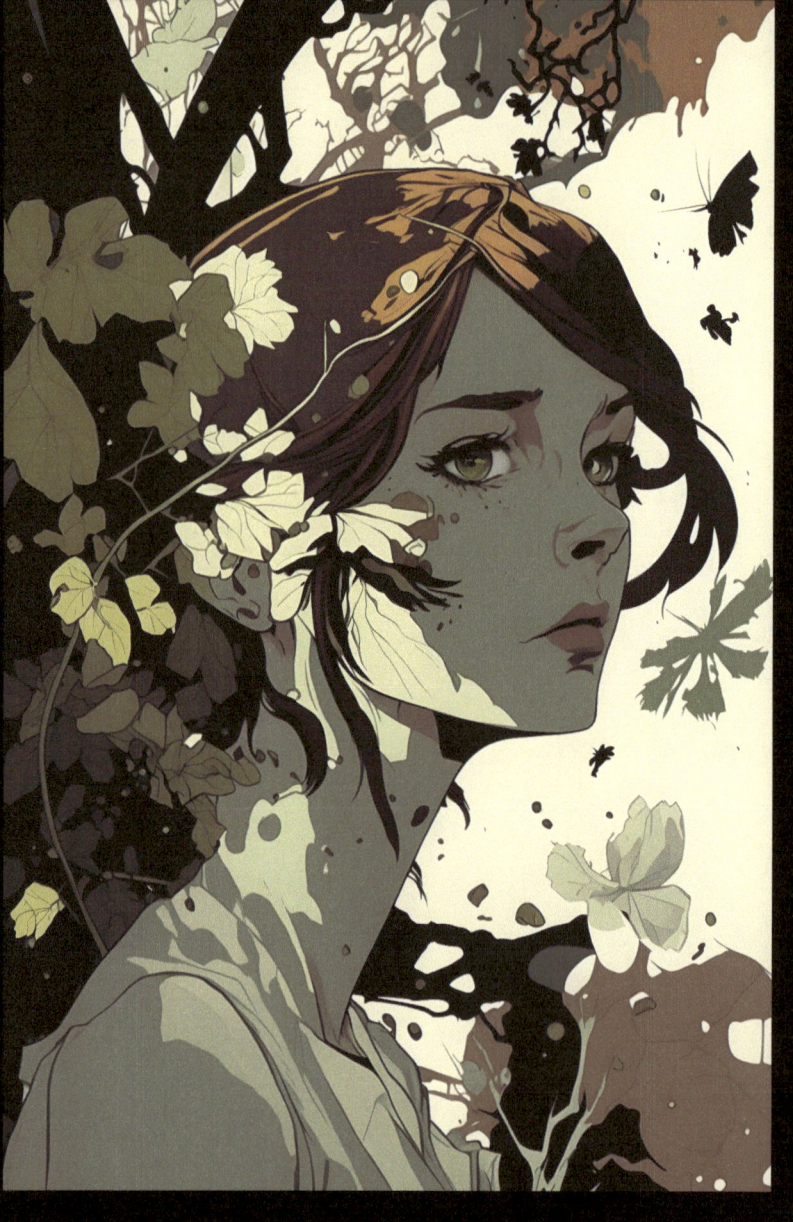

Human dreams are a canvas of the soul, where colors and shapes merge and intertwine in a dance of creativity.

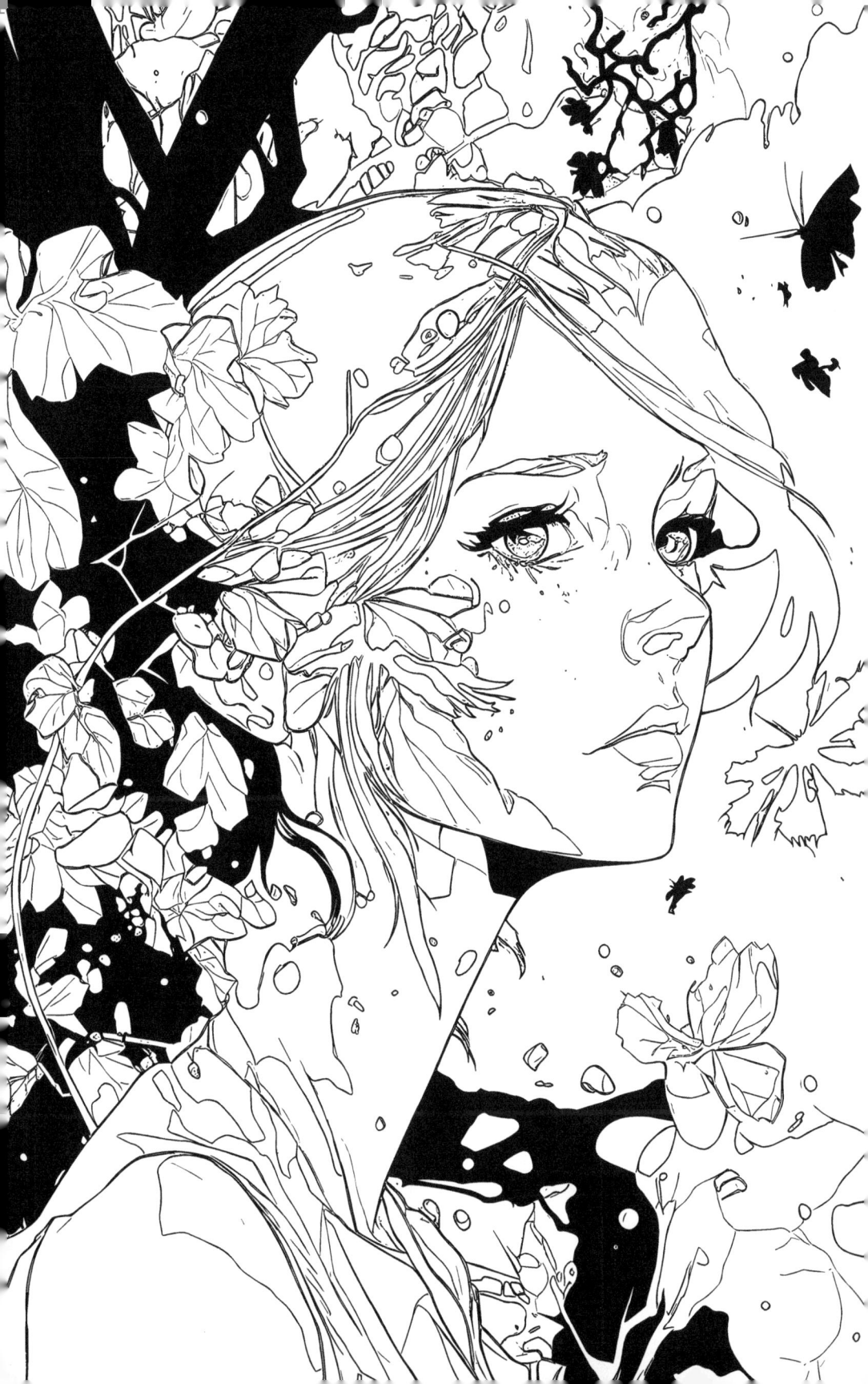

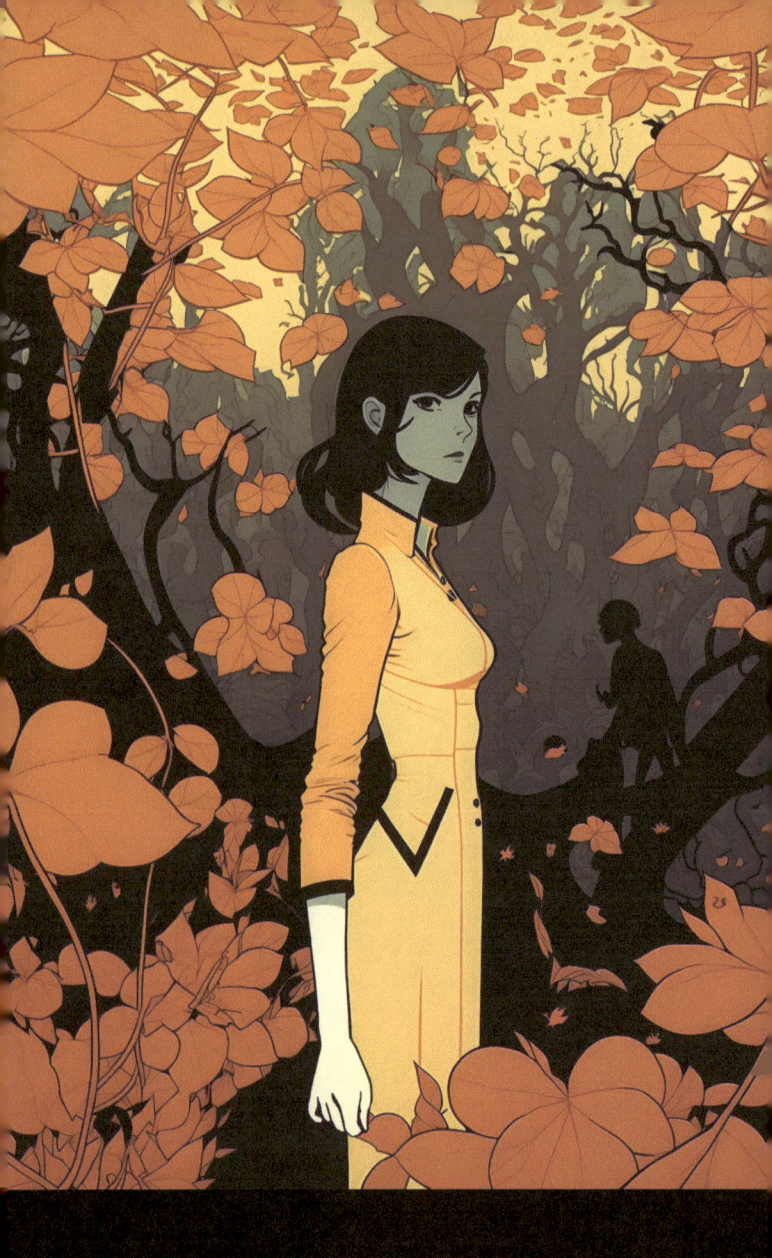

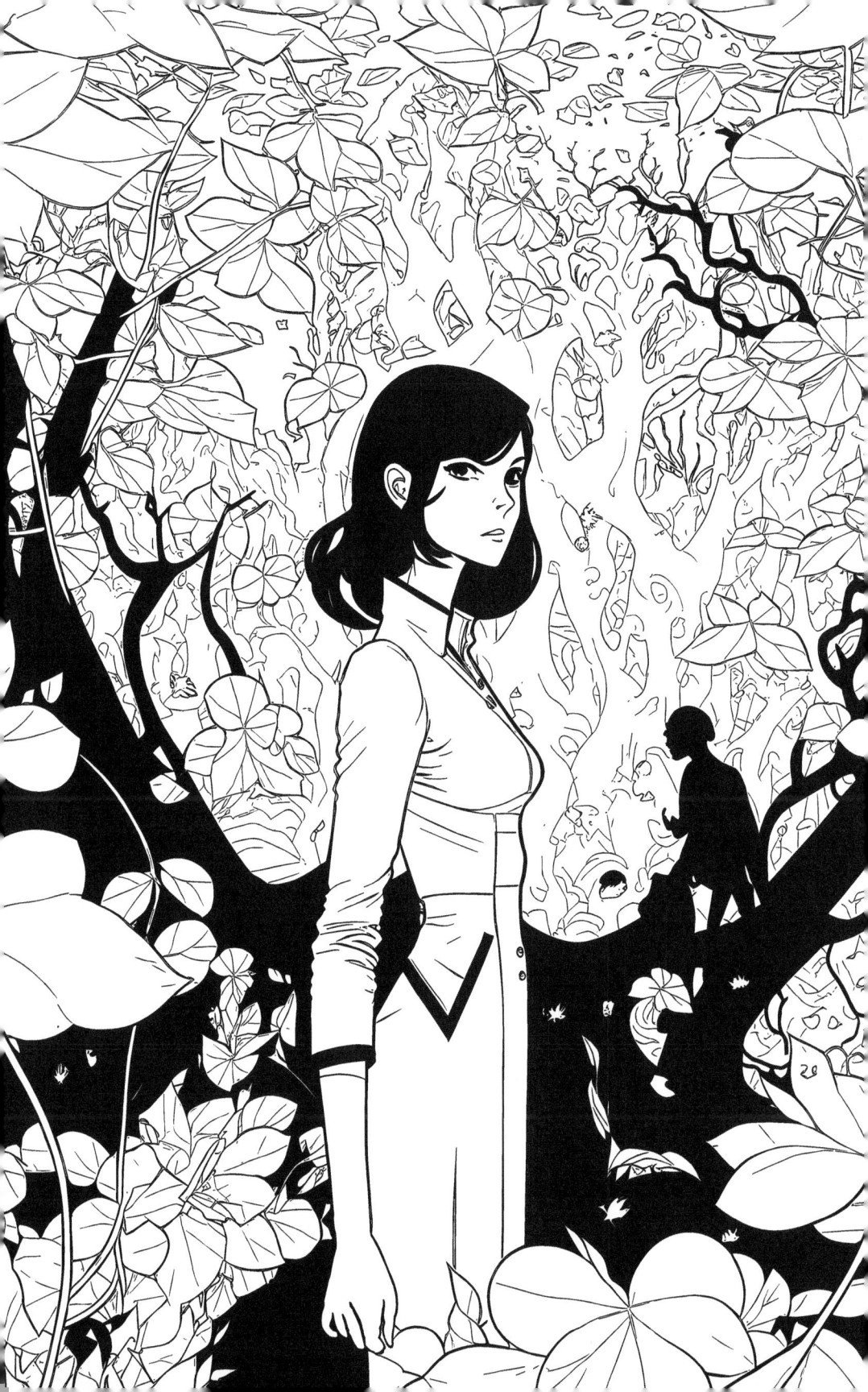

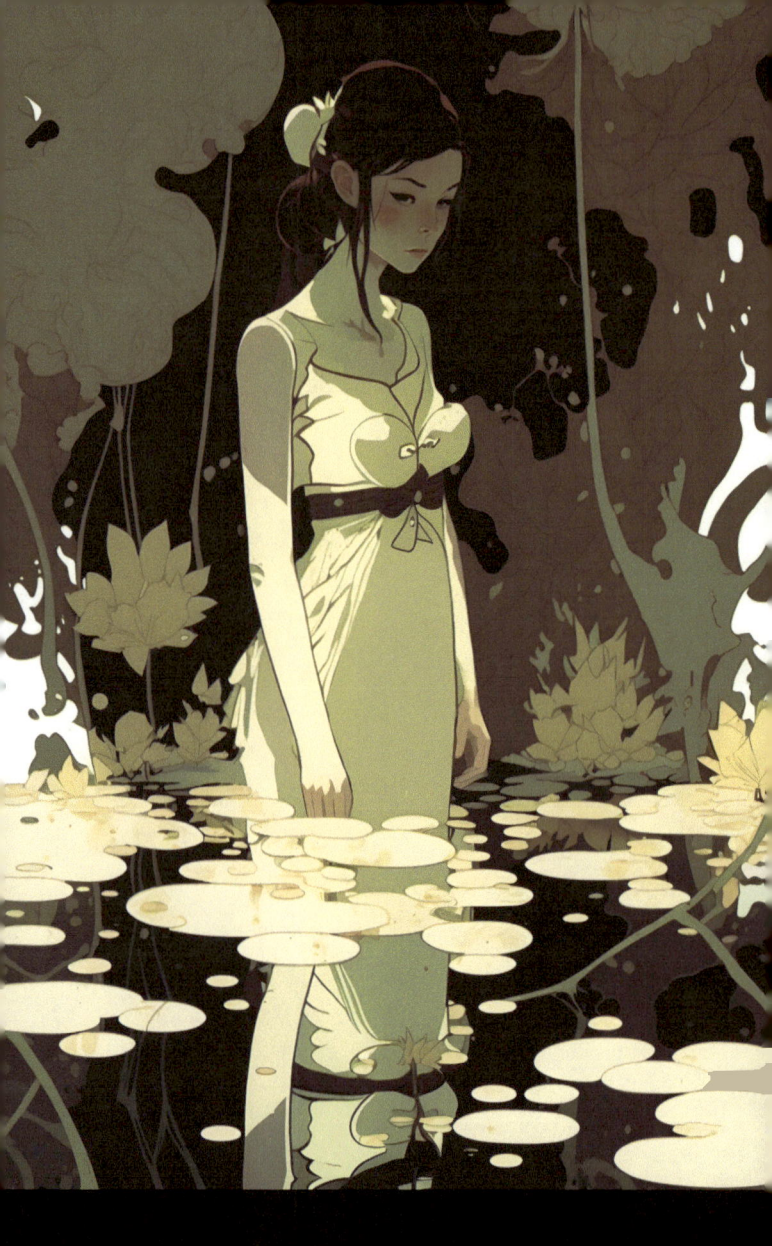

Each dream is a story waiting to be told, with the dreamer as both author and protagonist.

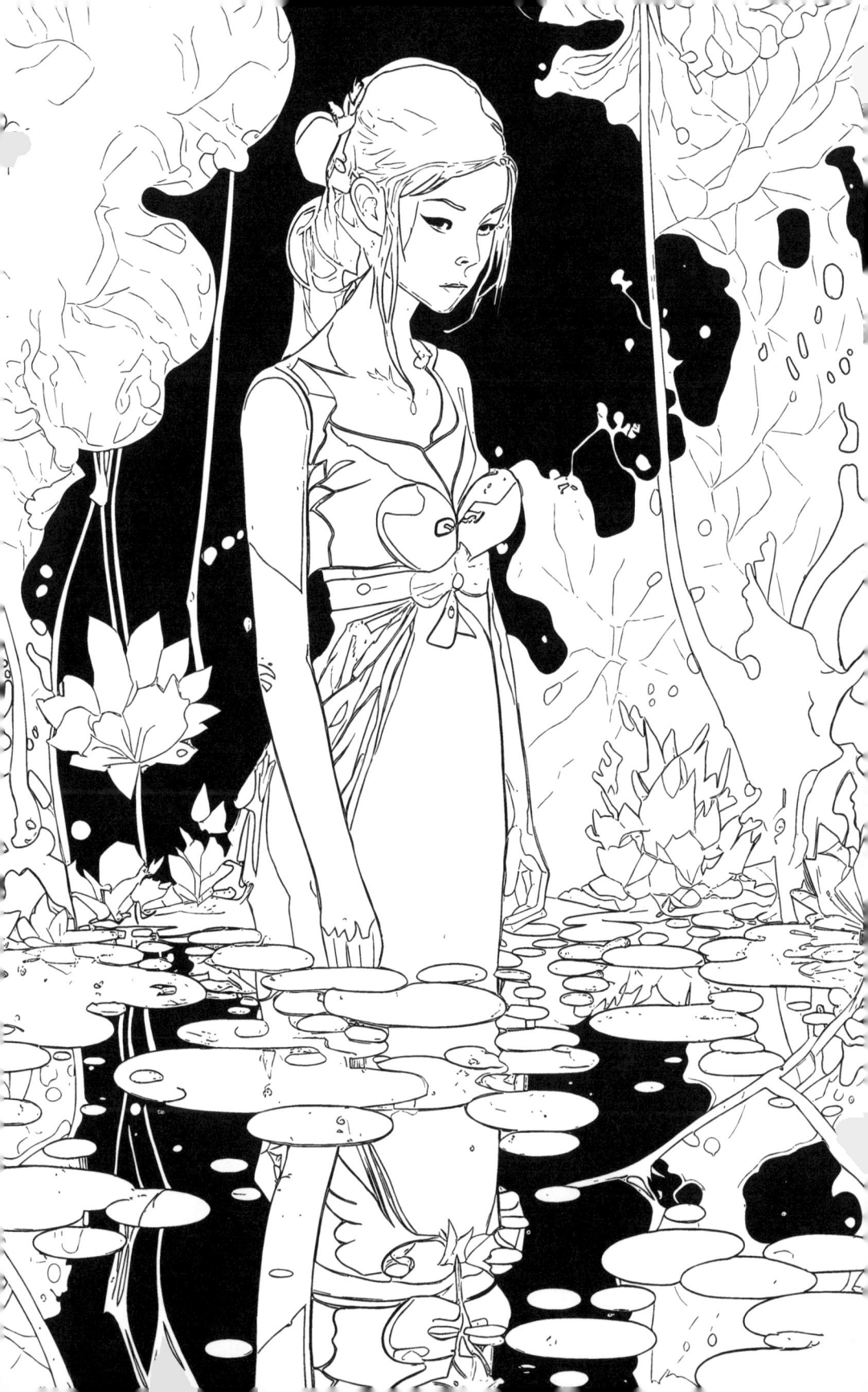

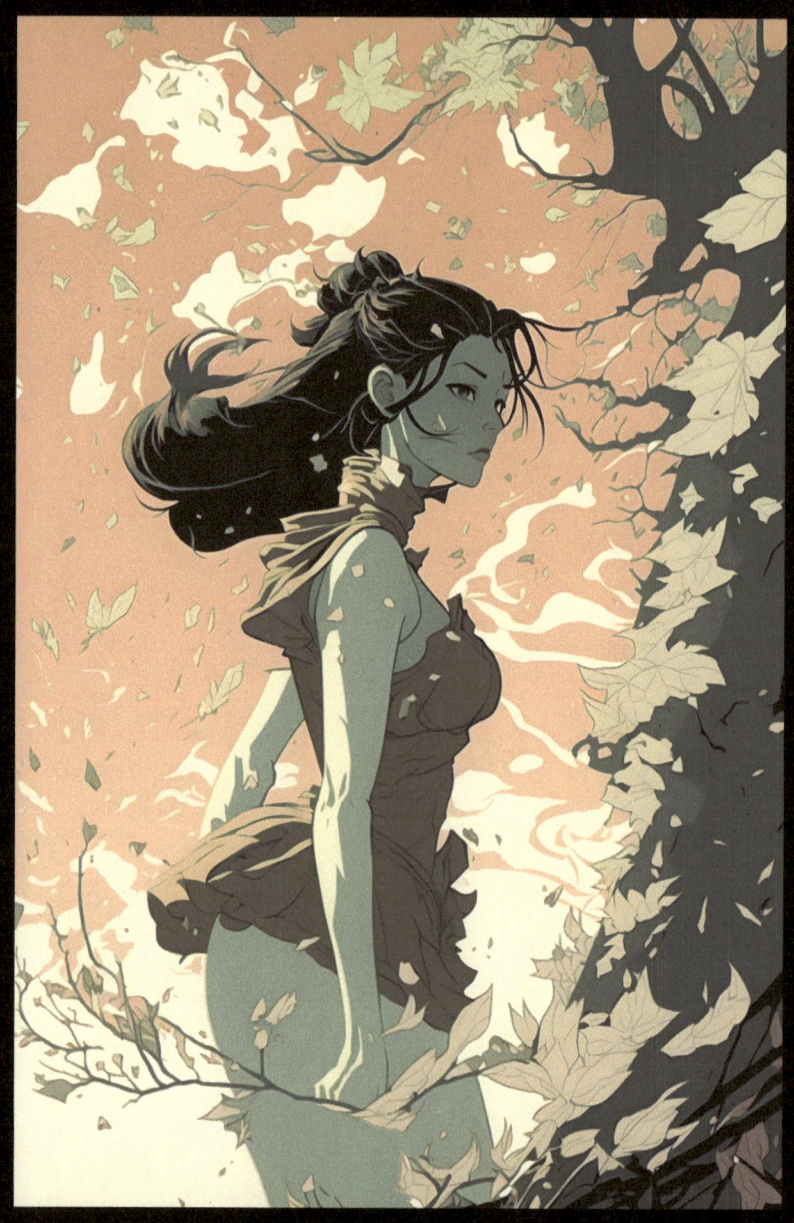

Chromatic dreams are the palette of the heart,
where shades and tones reflect the ebbs and flows of emotion.

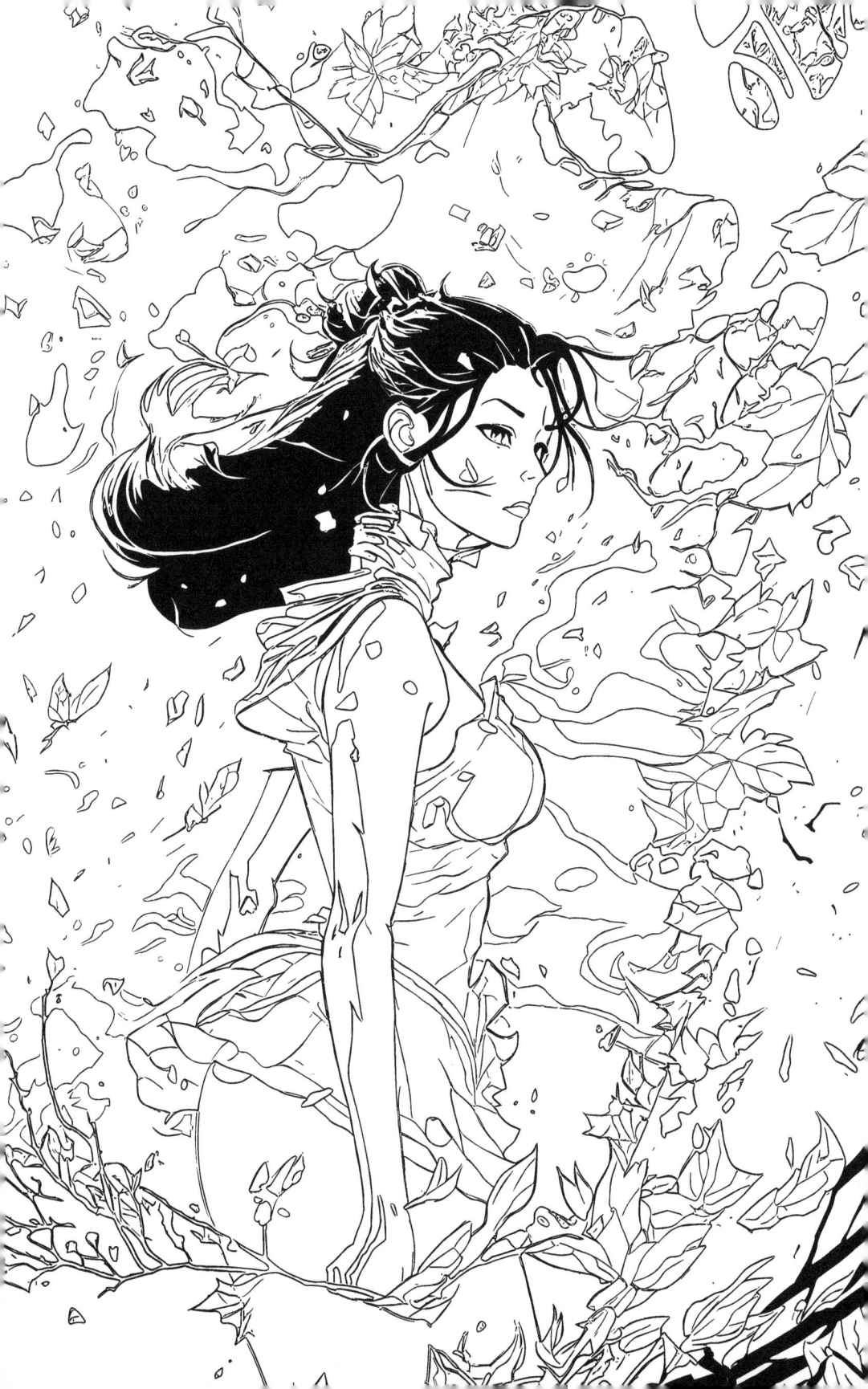

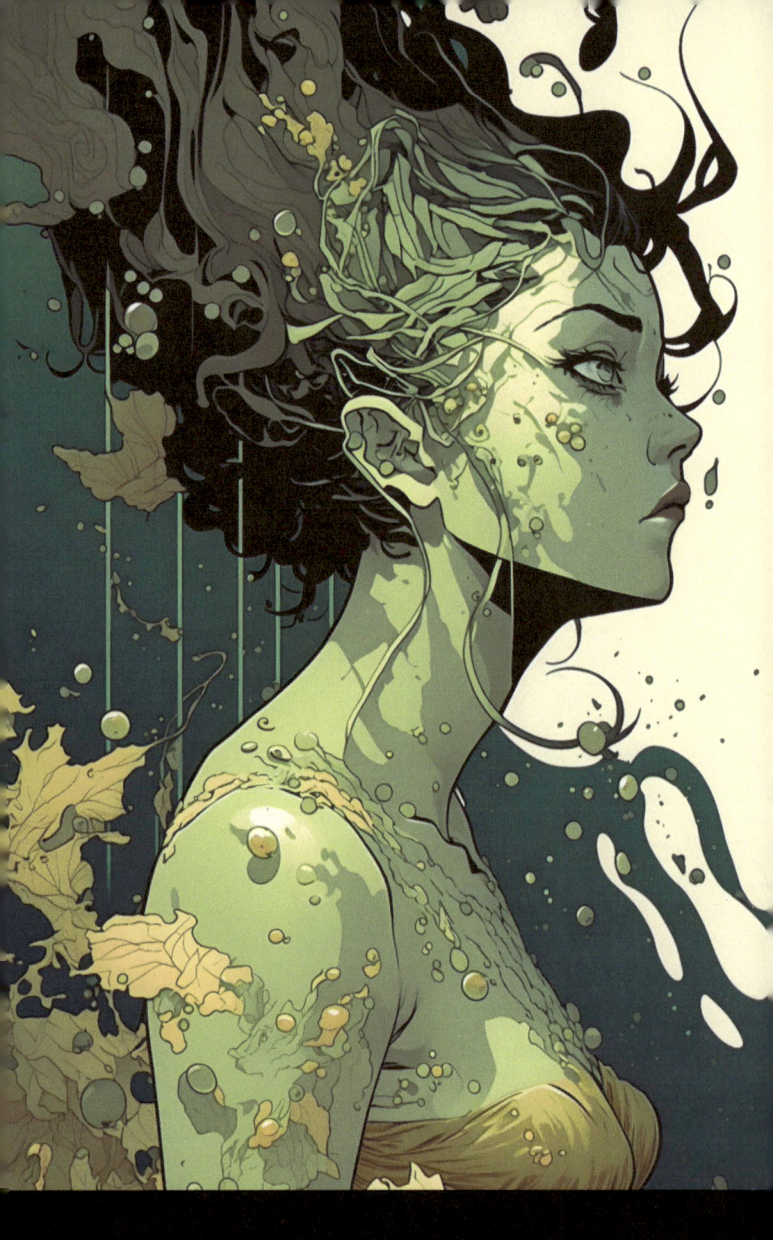

In the world of dreams, the impossible becomes possible and the mundane becomes magnificent.

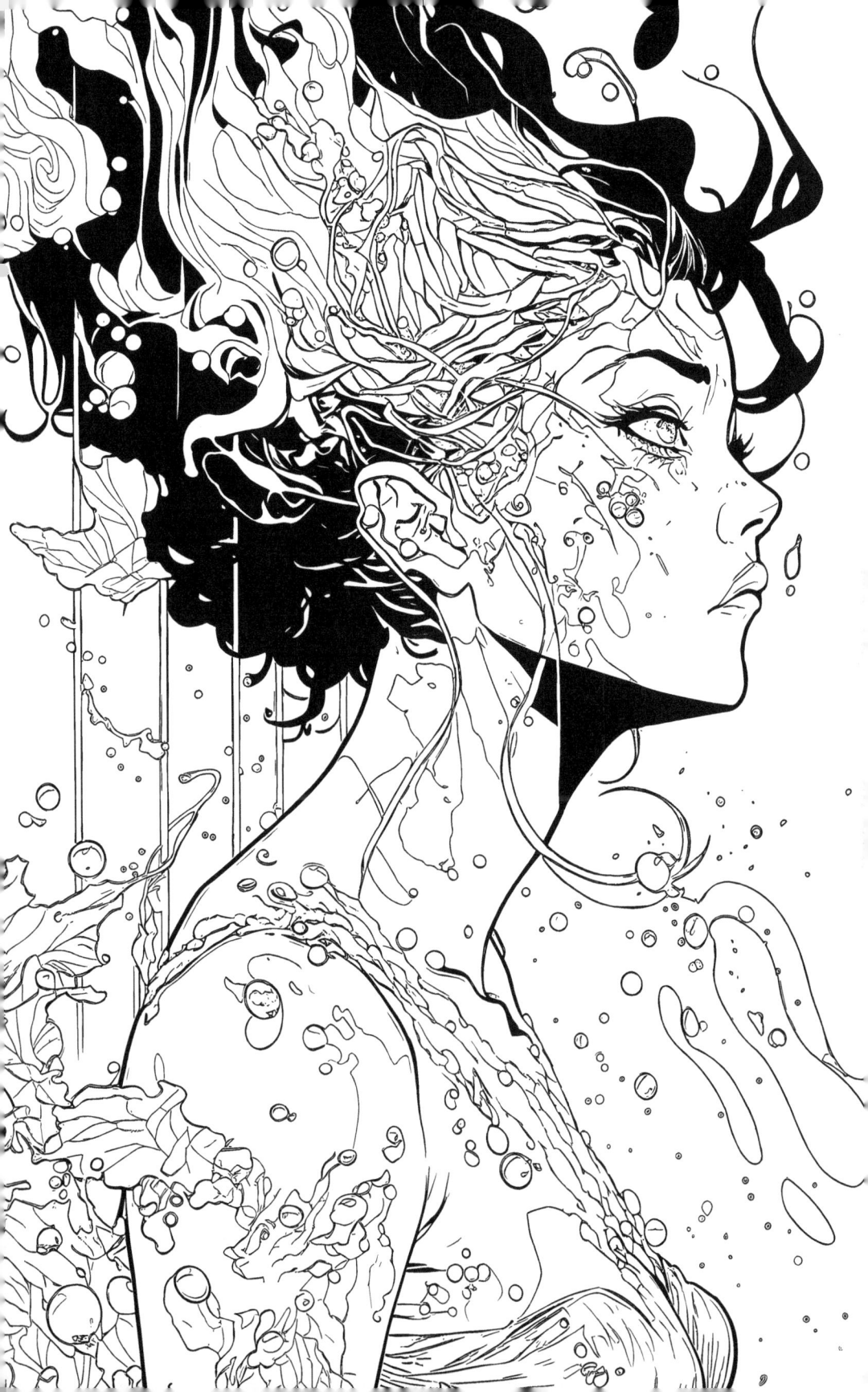

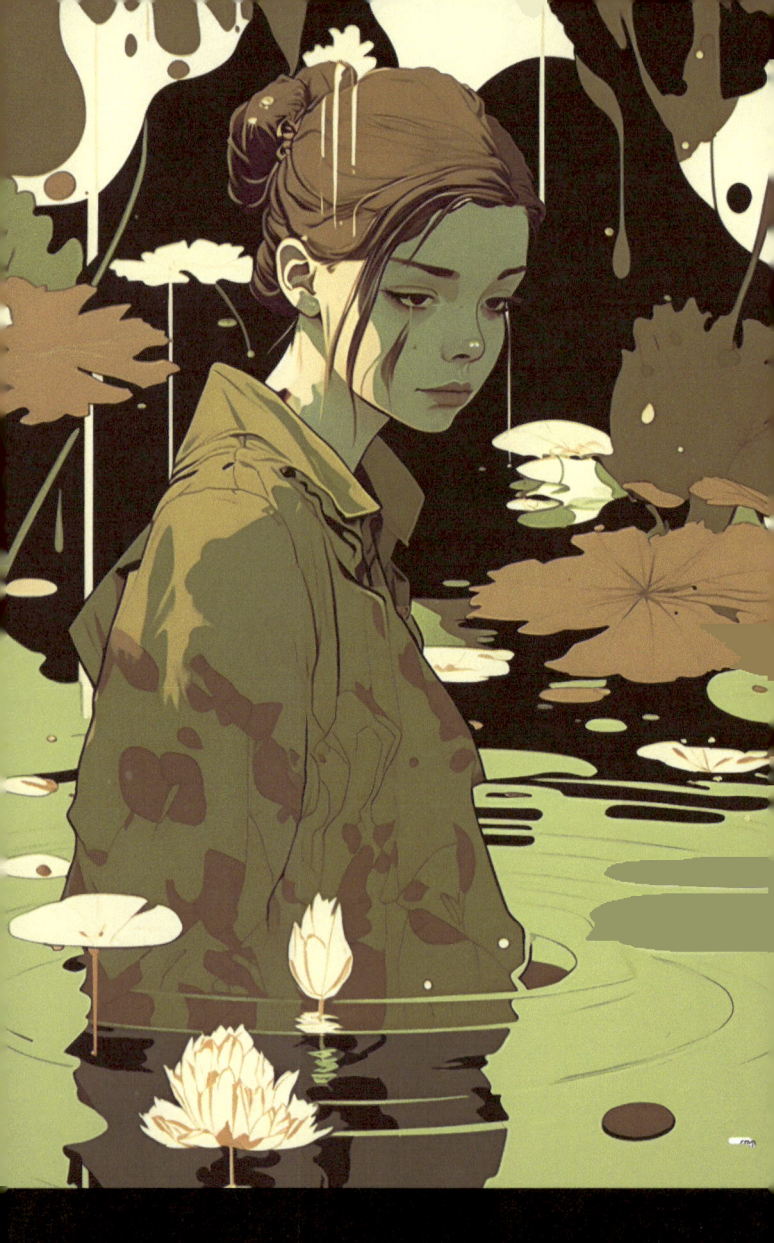

Each dream is a melody waiting to be heard, with the dreamer as both composer and conductor.

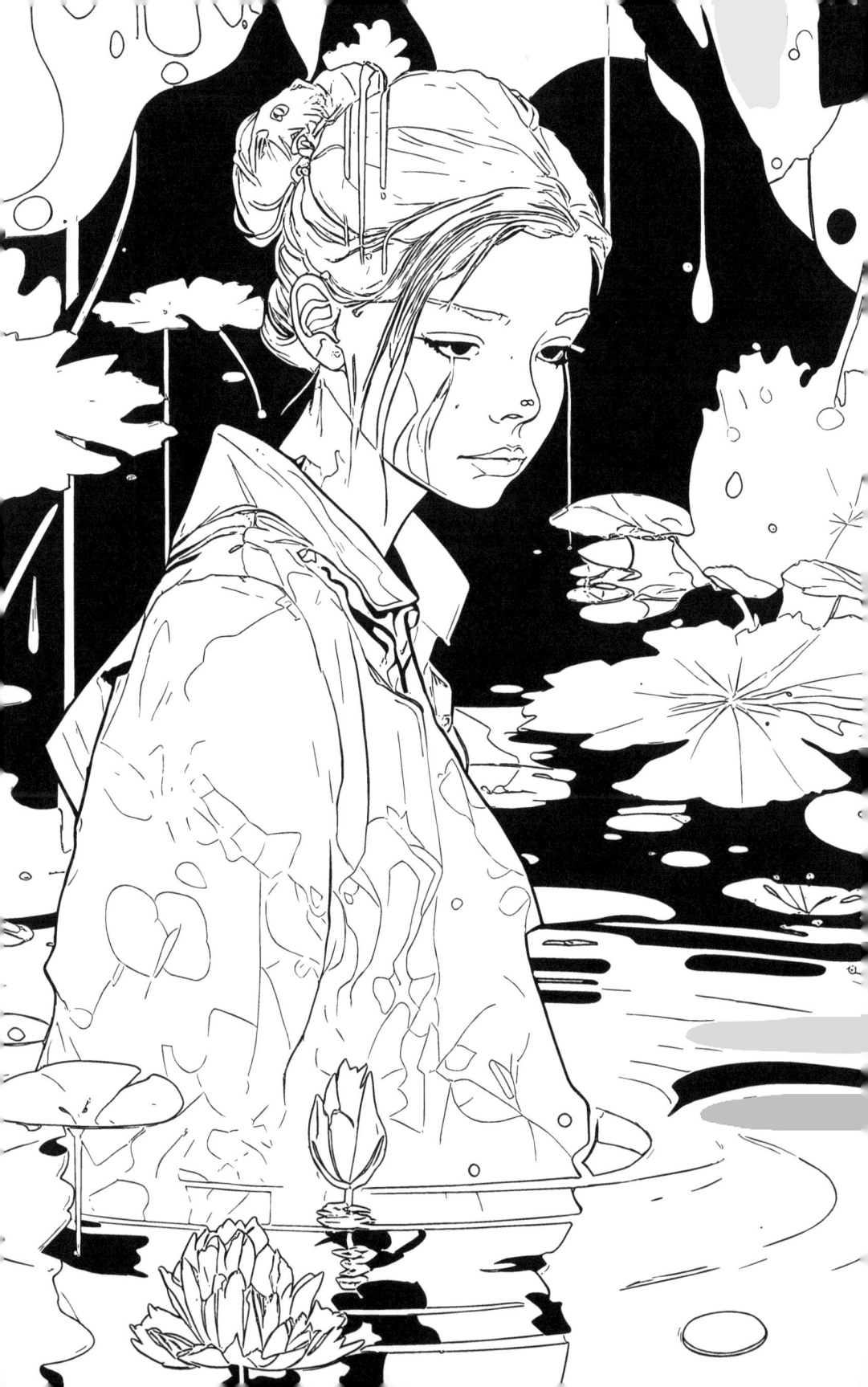

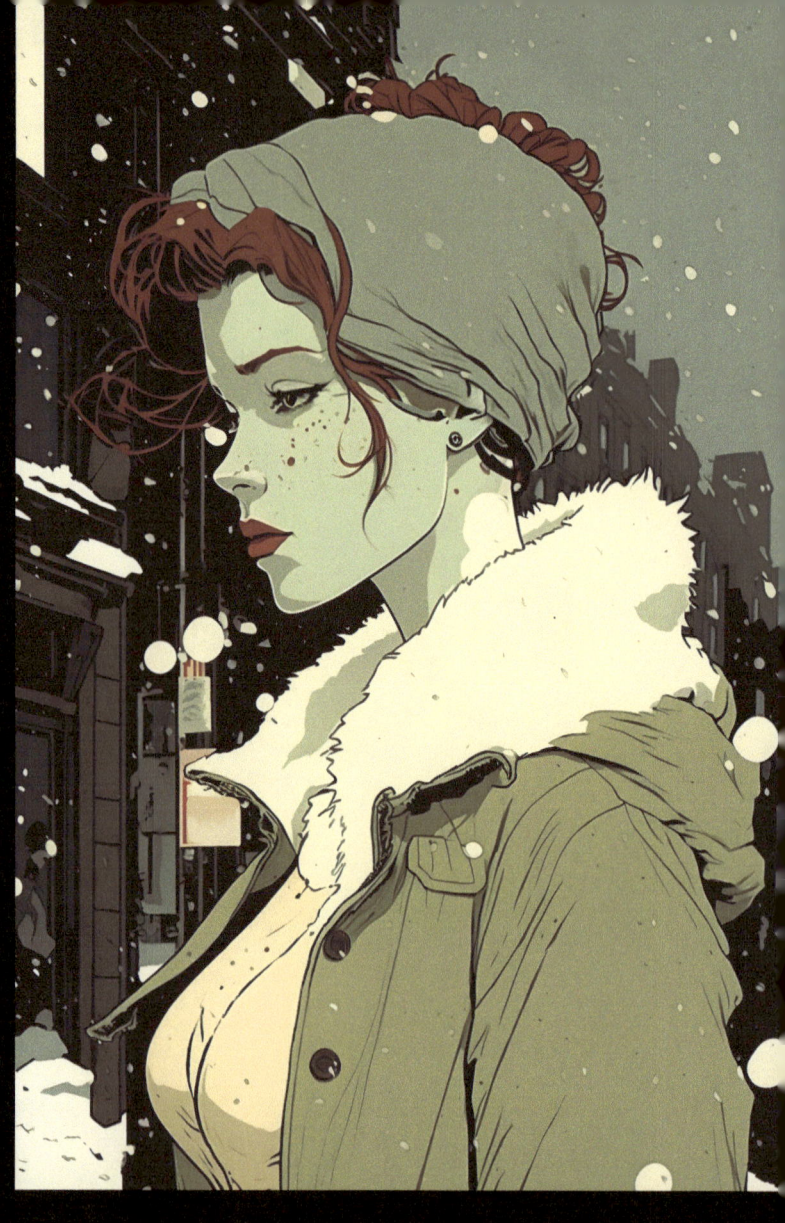

The world of dreams is a canvas of the soul, where the brushstrokes of the imagination create a masterpiece of the self.

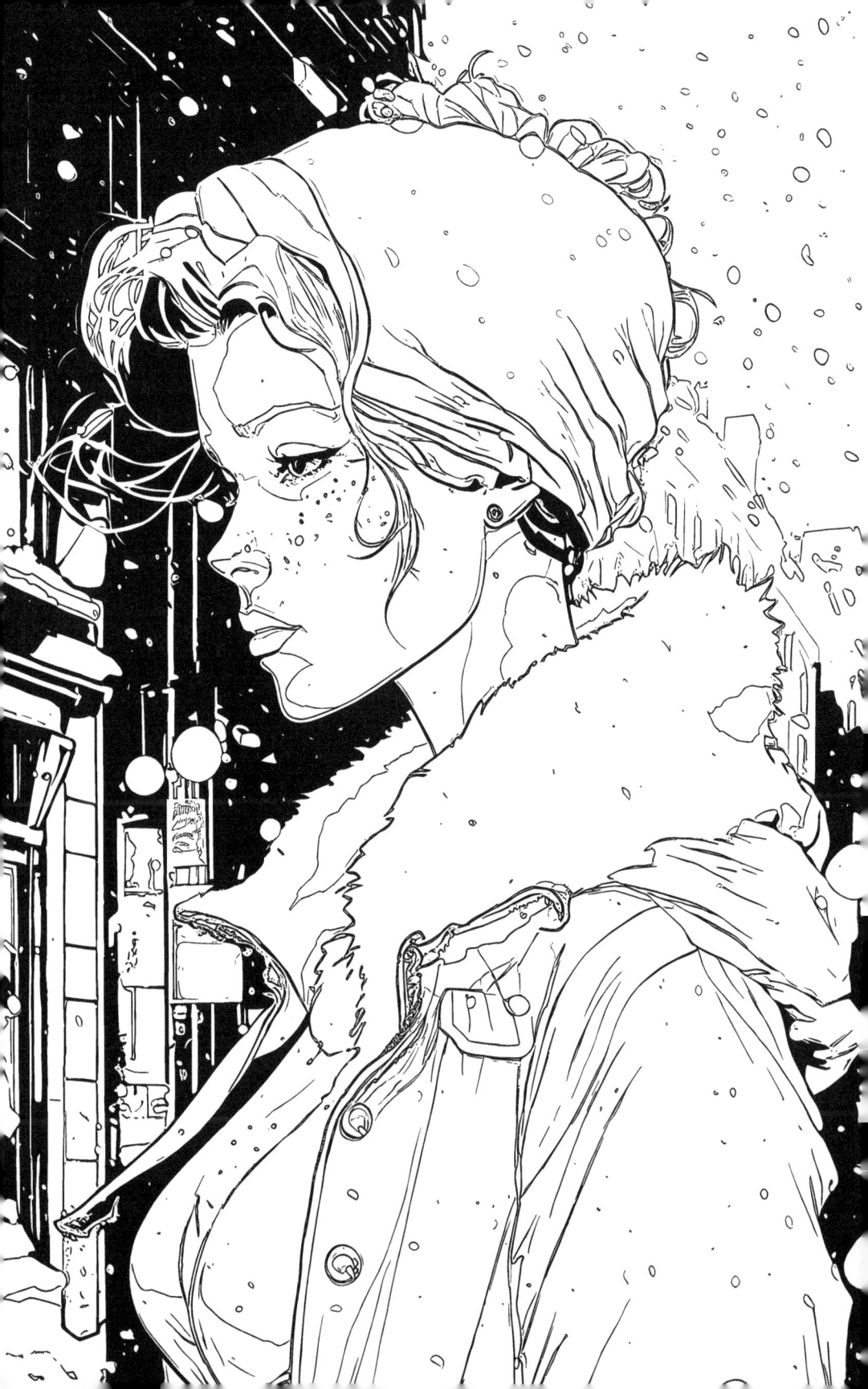

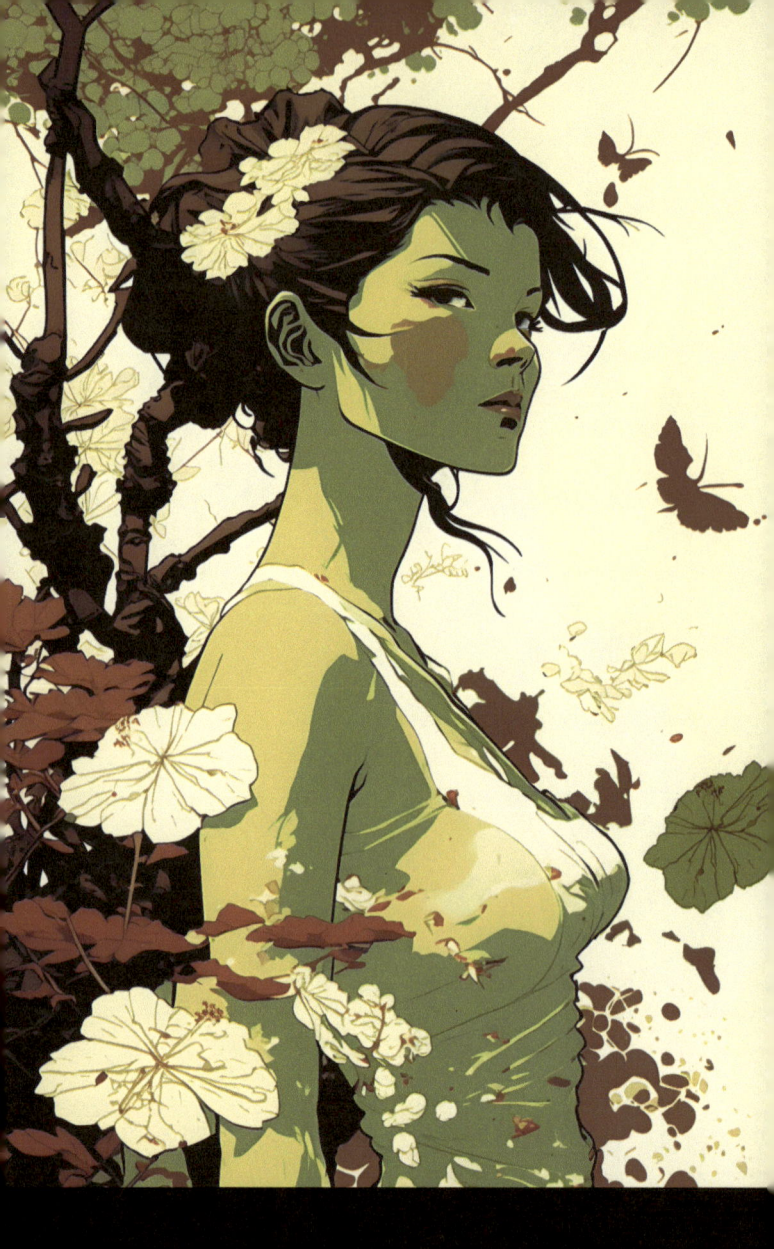

In the world of dreams, the innermost desires and fears are revealed, becoming part of the conscious experience.

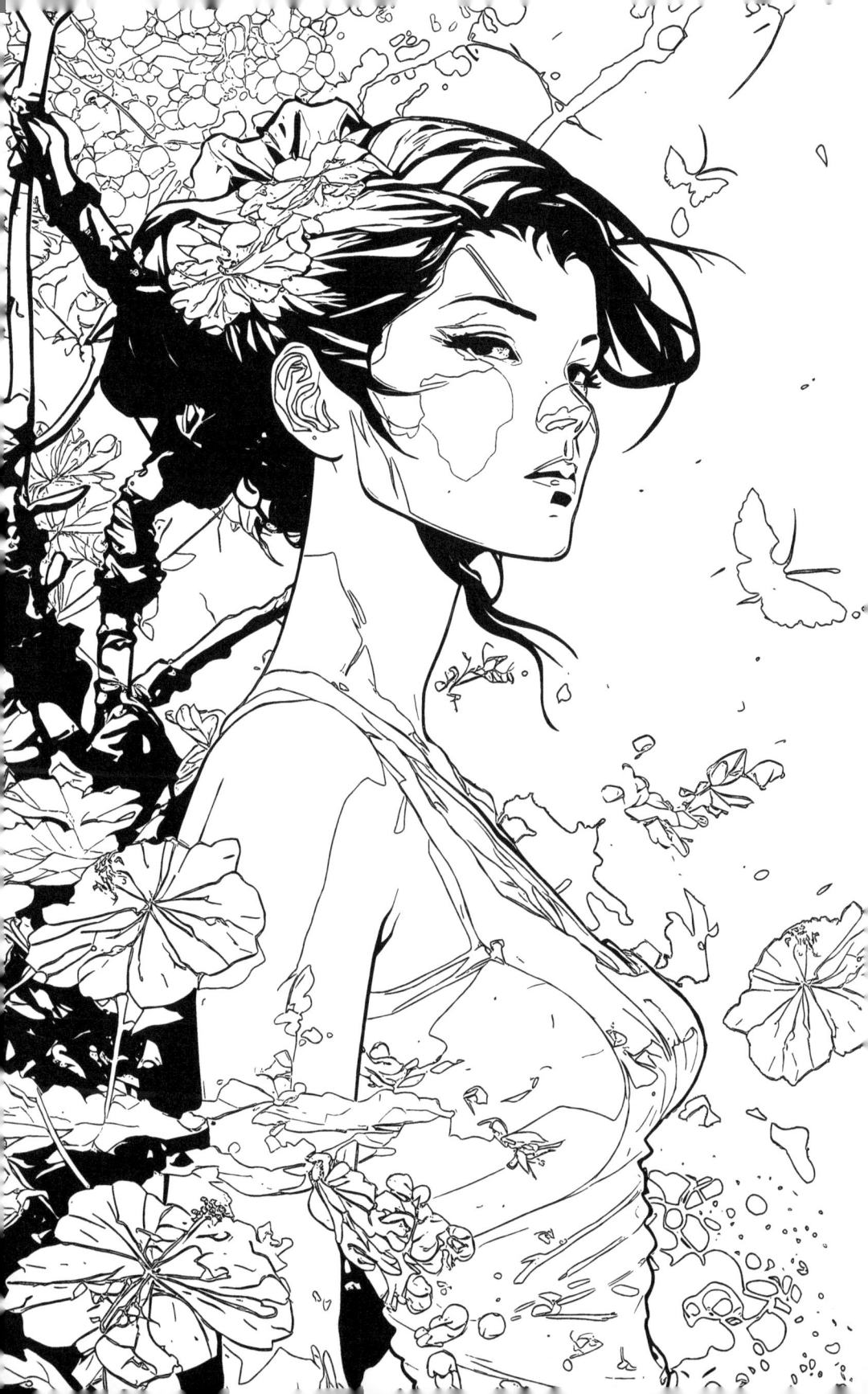

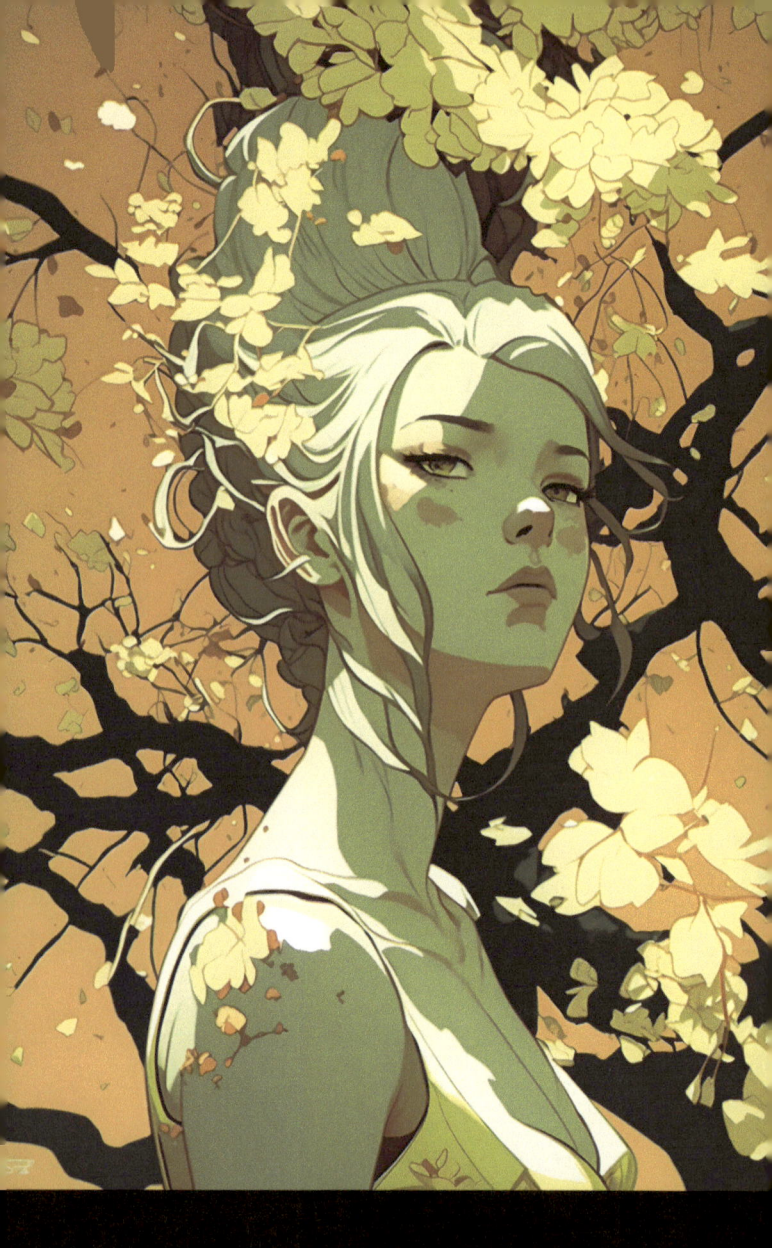

Dreams are the palette of the mind, where emotions and thoughts are expressed in vivid colors and tones.

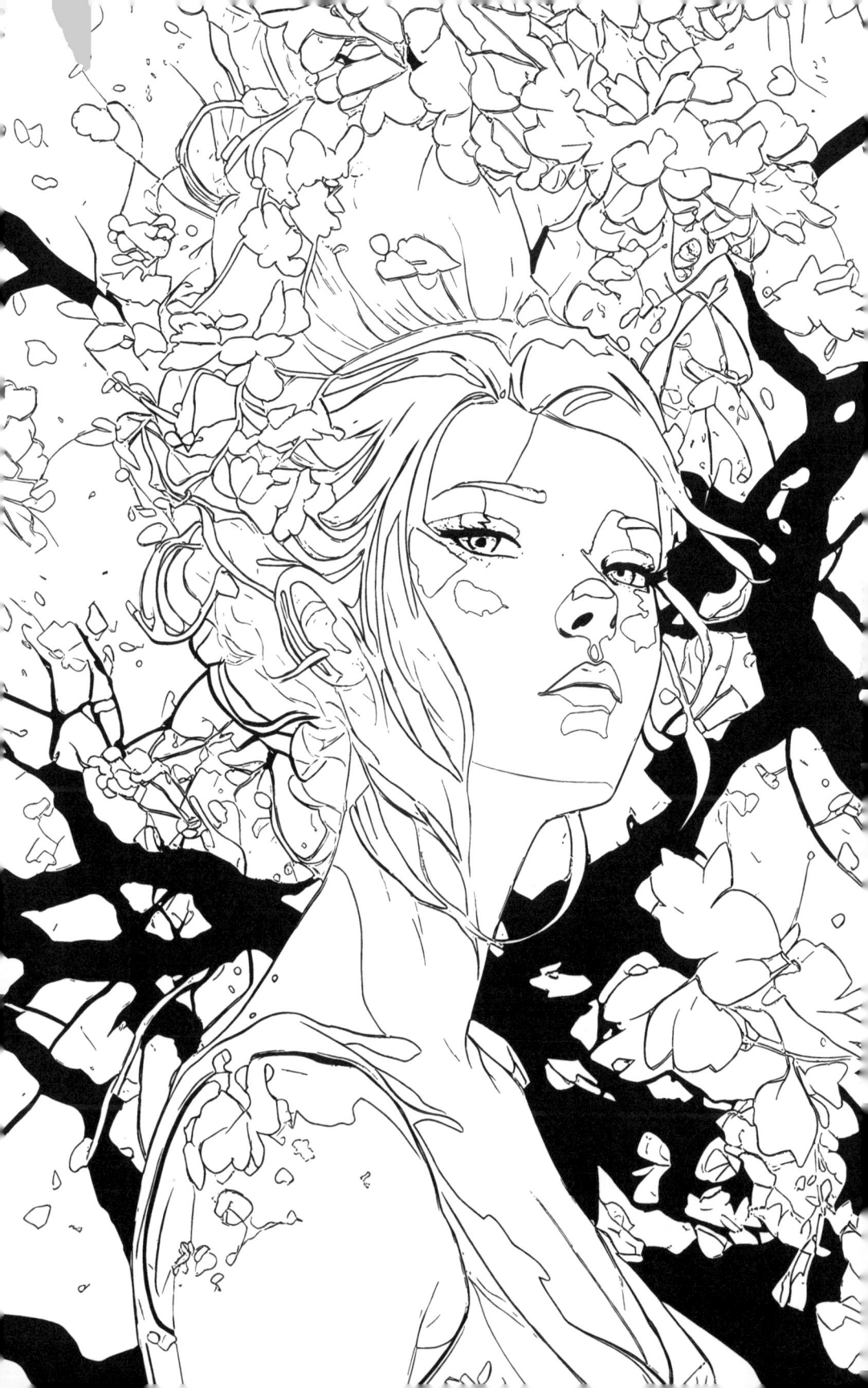

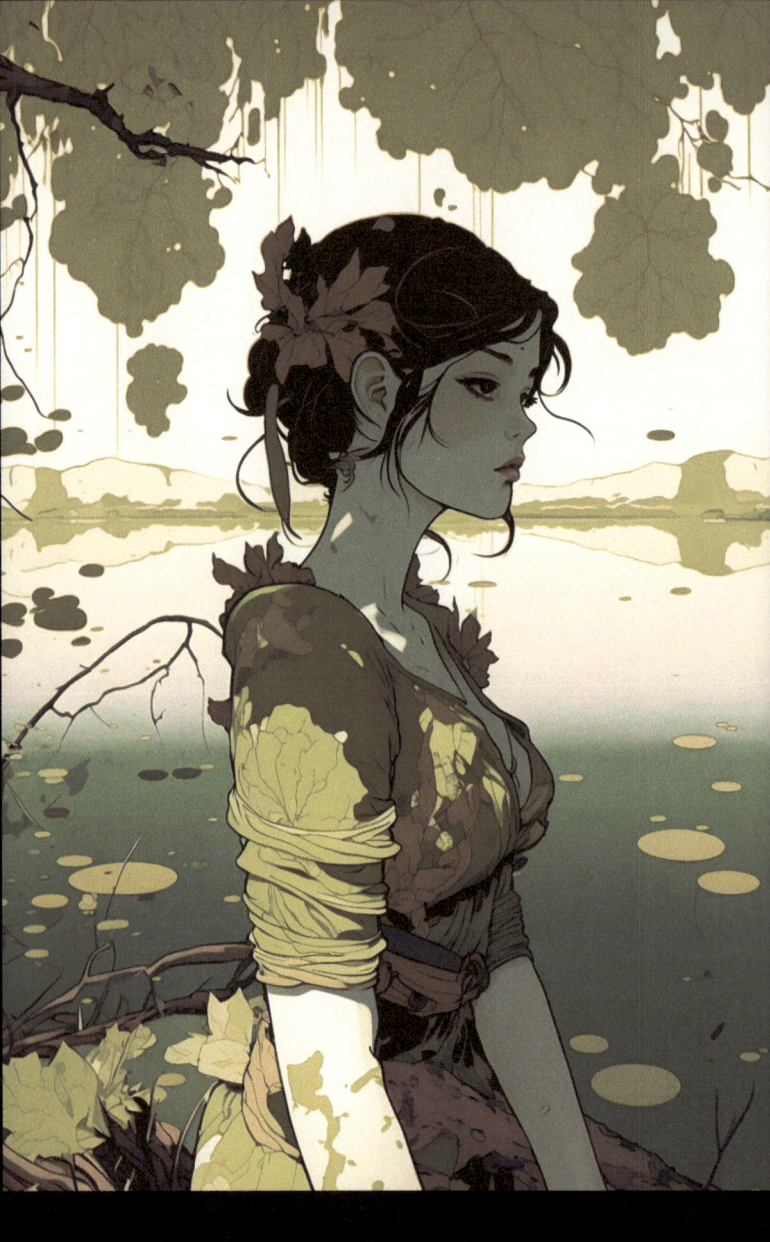

The unconscious is a vast ocean of the self, and dreams are the waves that stir it to life.

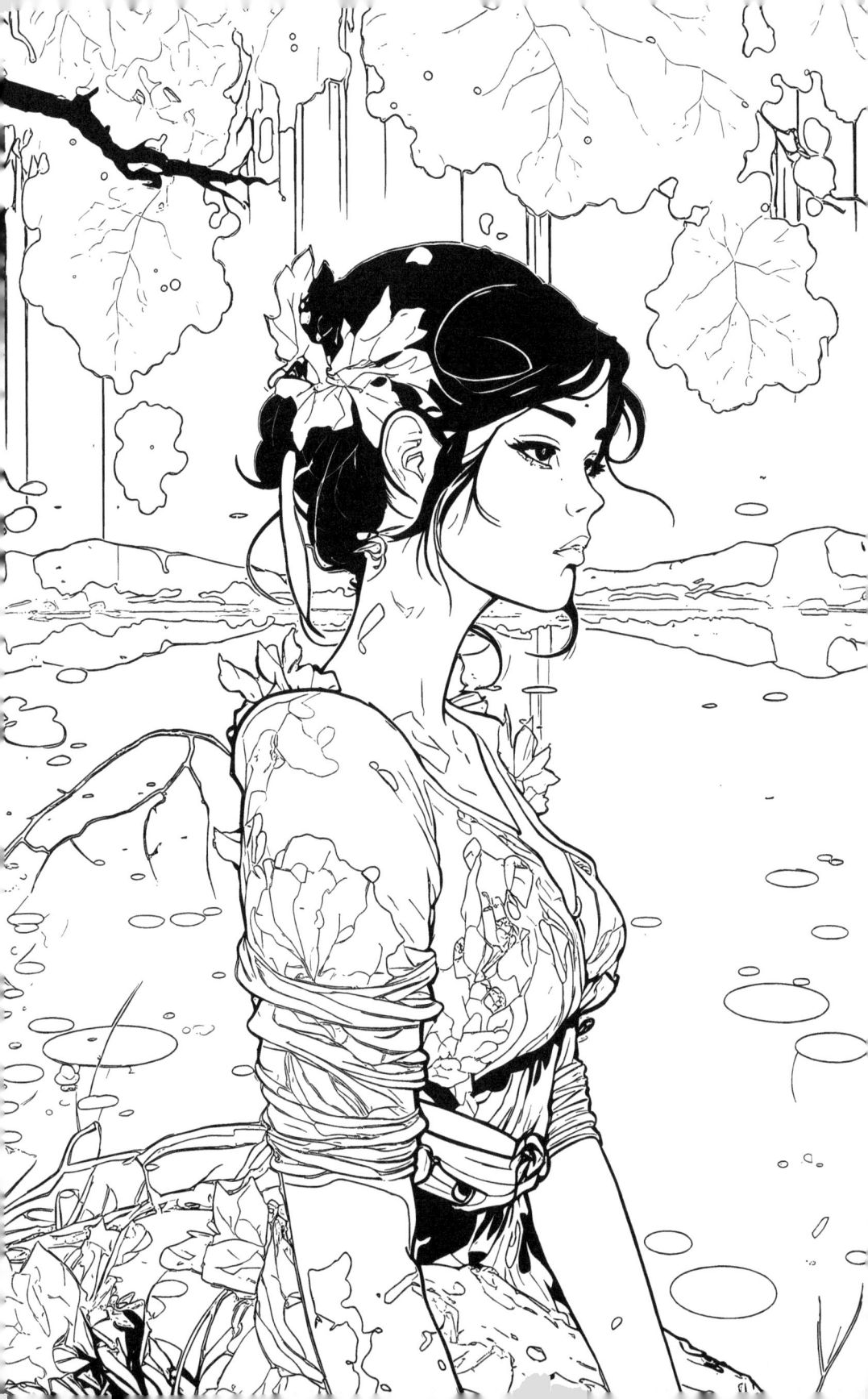

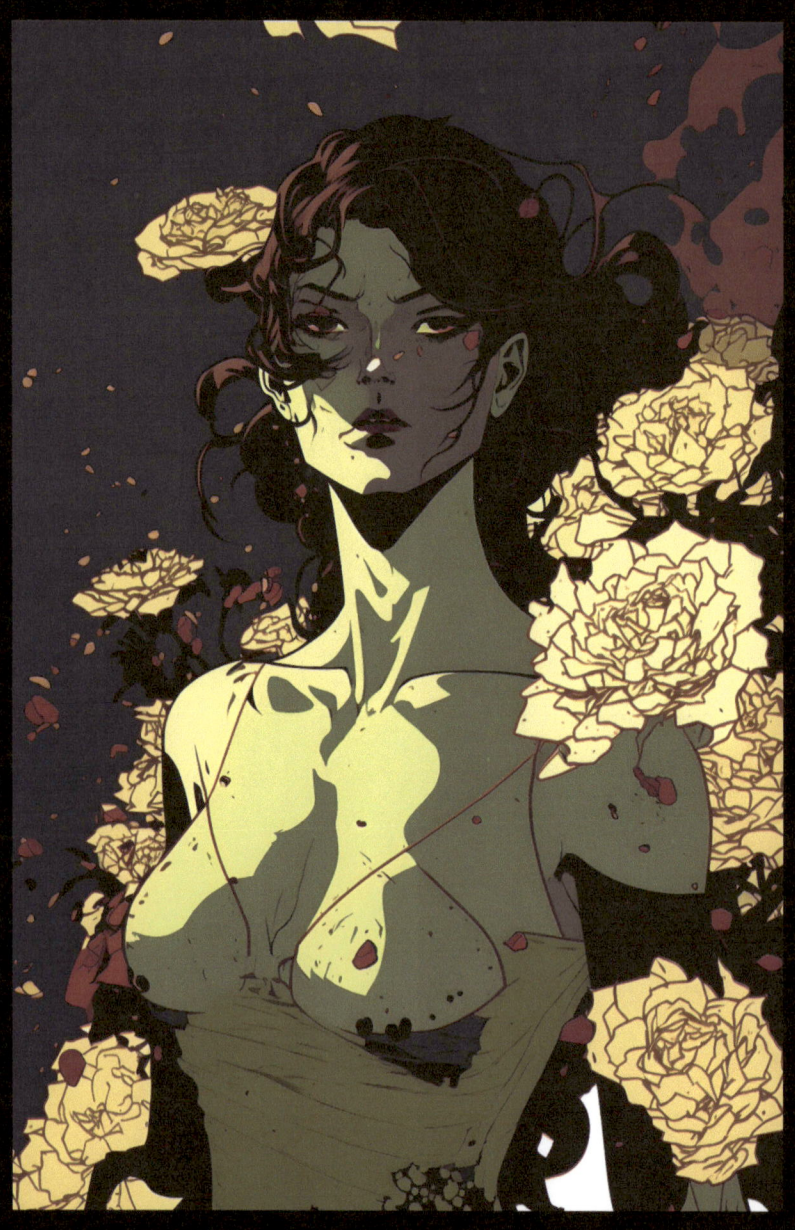

Nighttime is the canvas on which our subconscious paints its secrets.

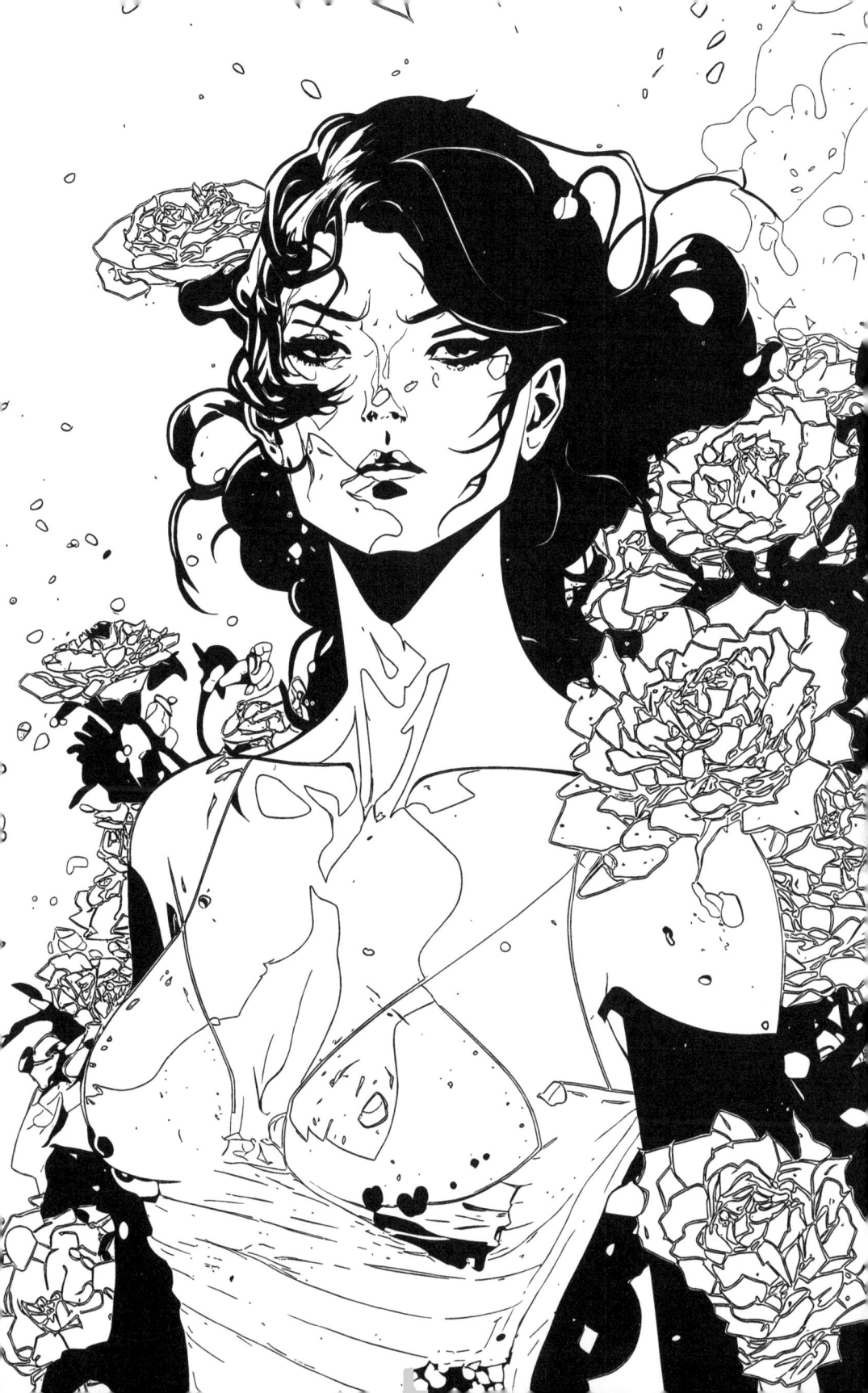

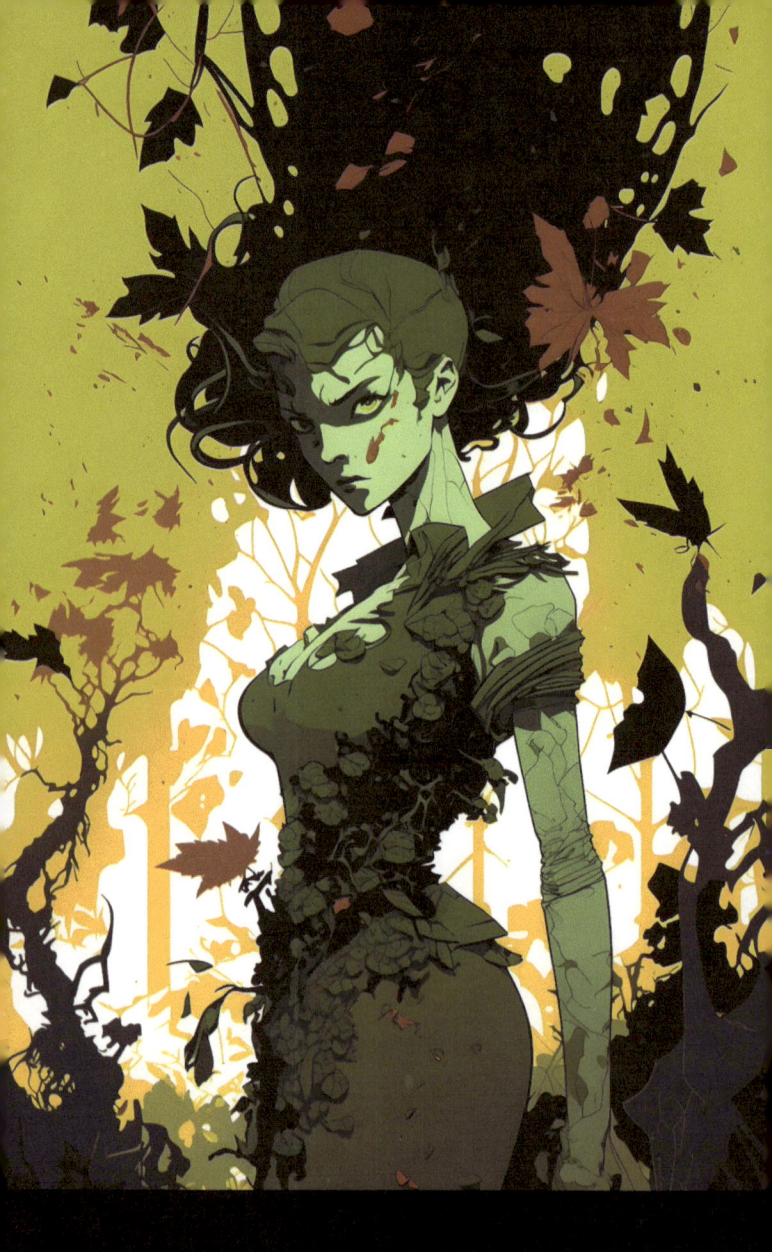

Chromatic dreams are the gallery of the heart, where each image is a masterpiece of emotion.

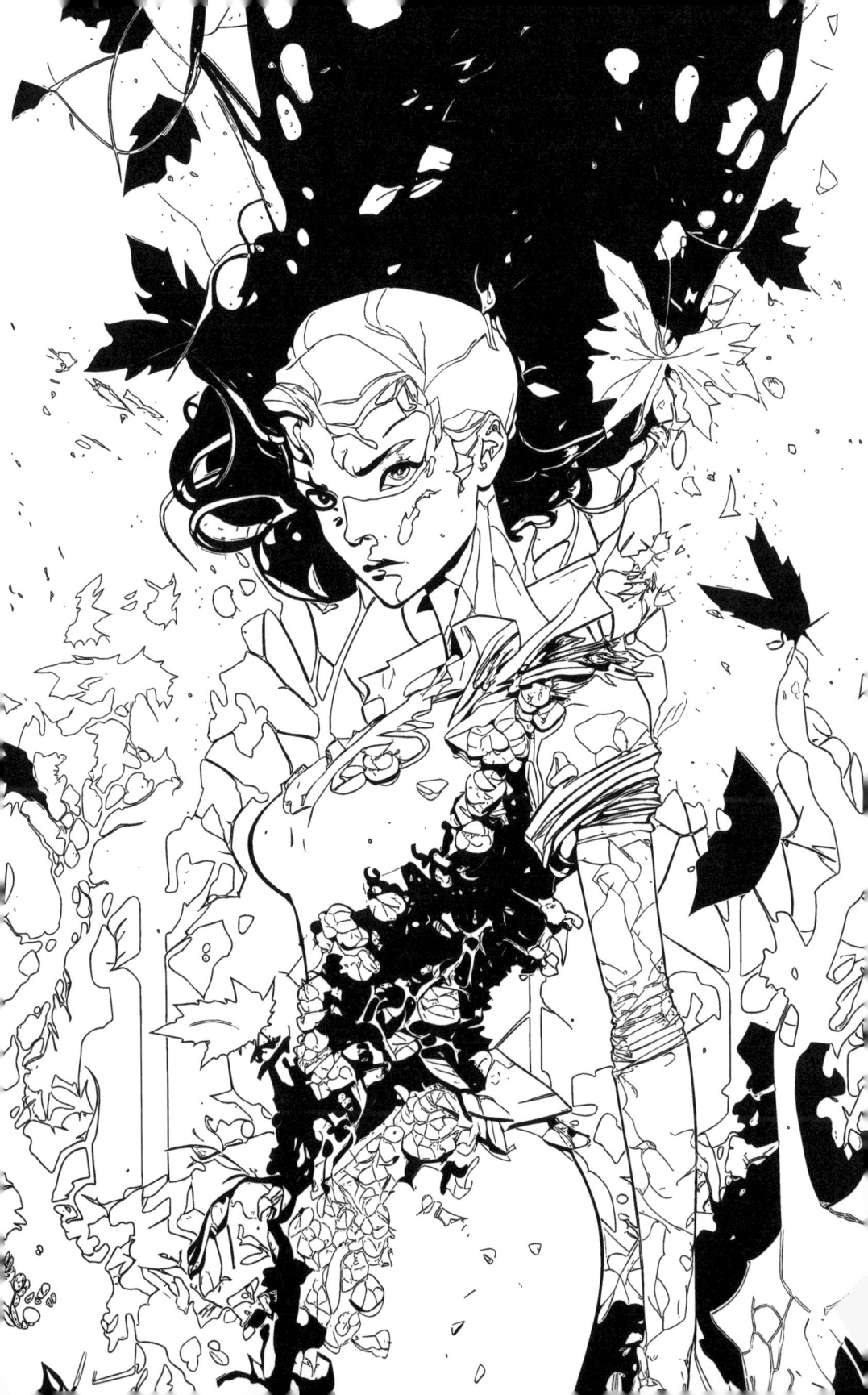

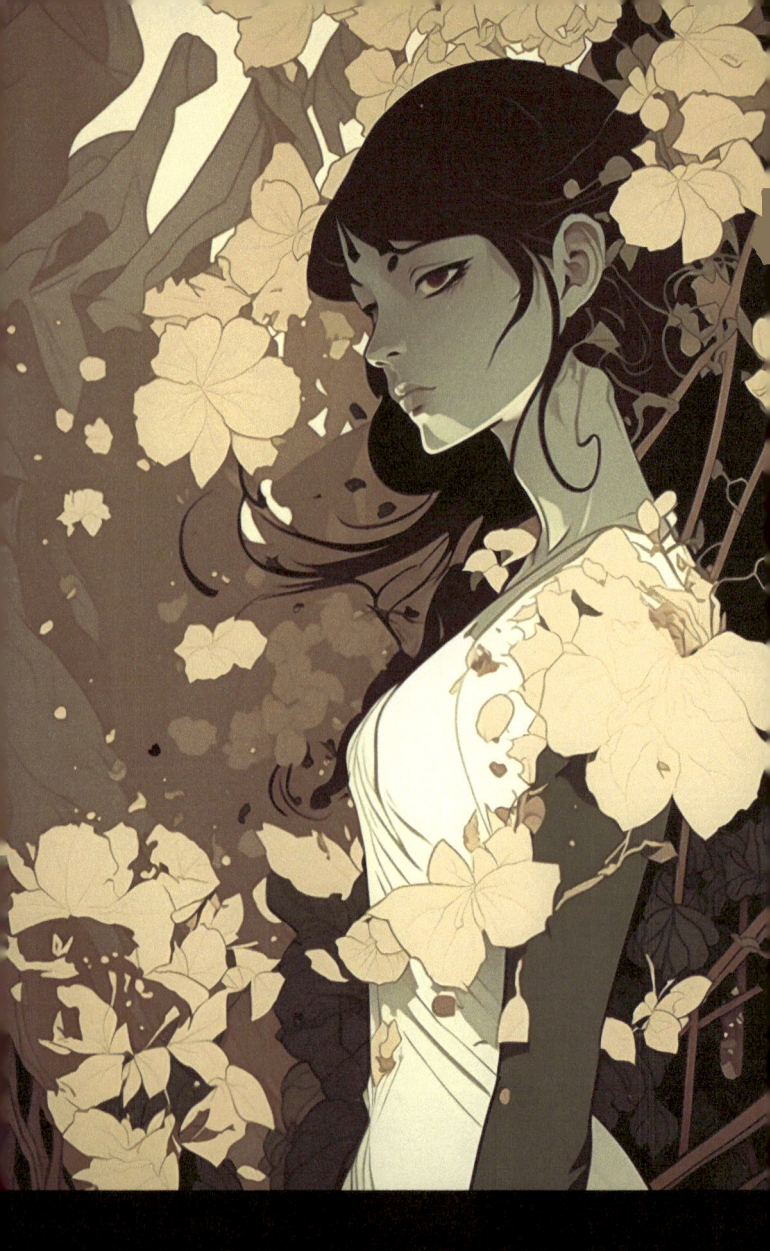

The art of dreaming is a dance of the imagination, where creativity and inspiration take center stage.

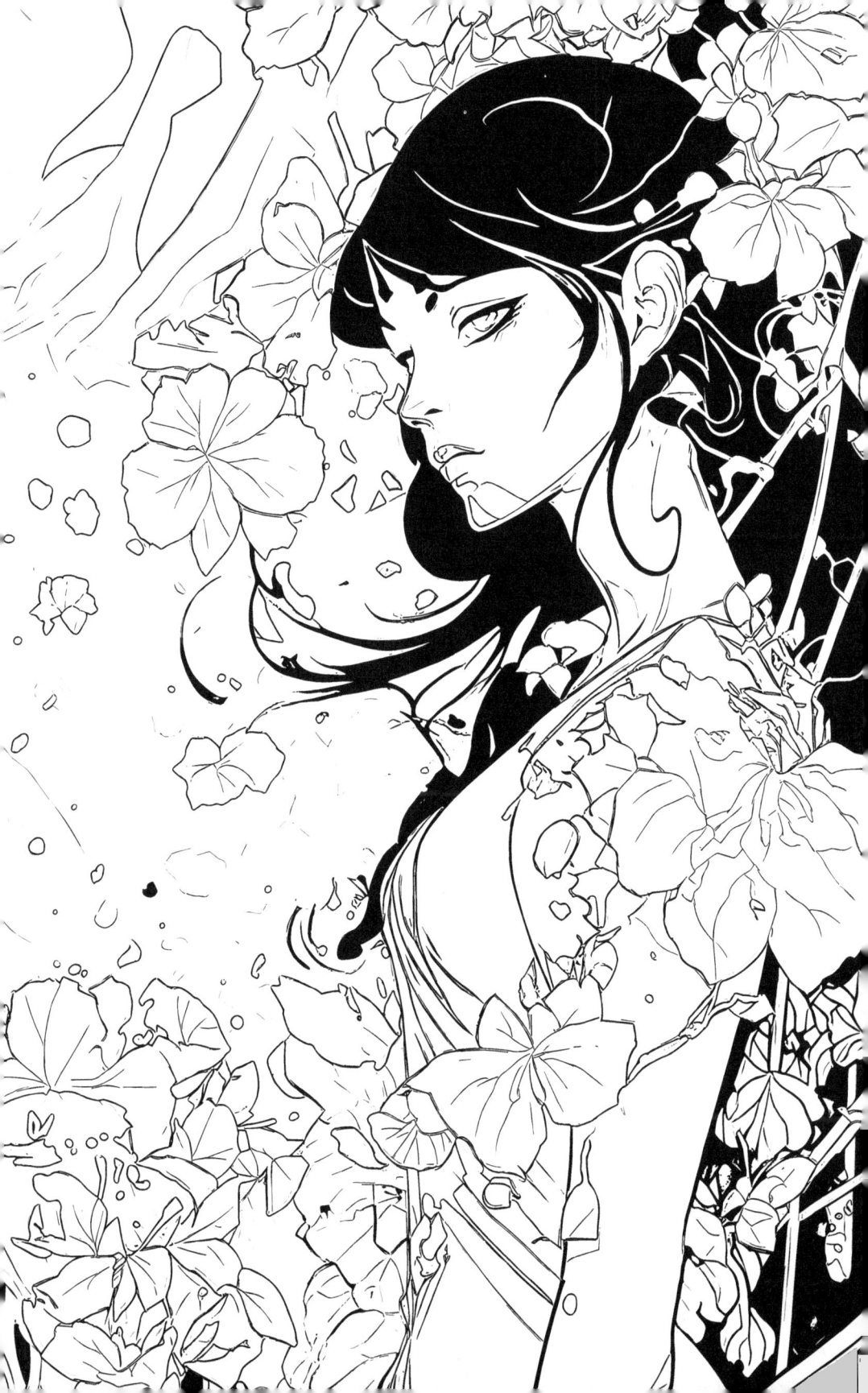

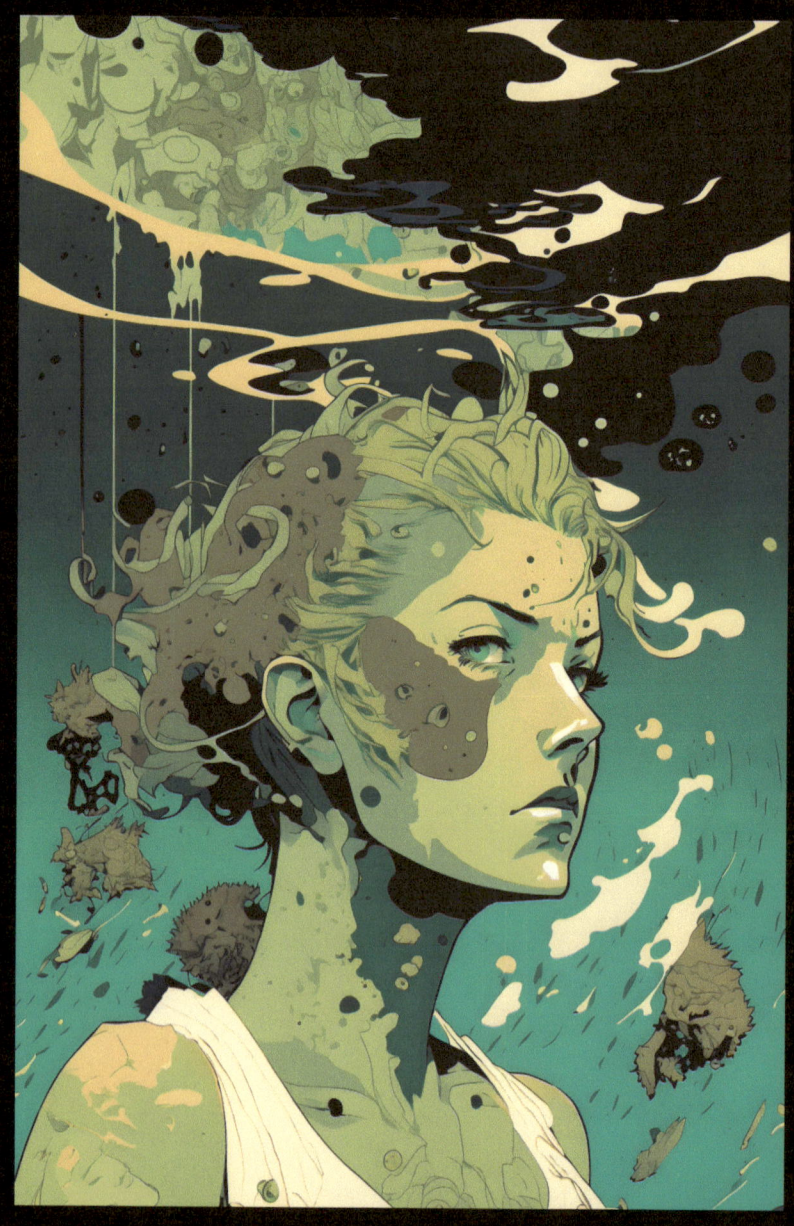

Dreams are a reminder that anything is possible, if only we dare to dream.

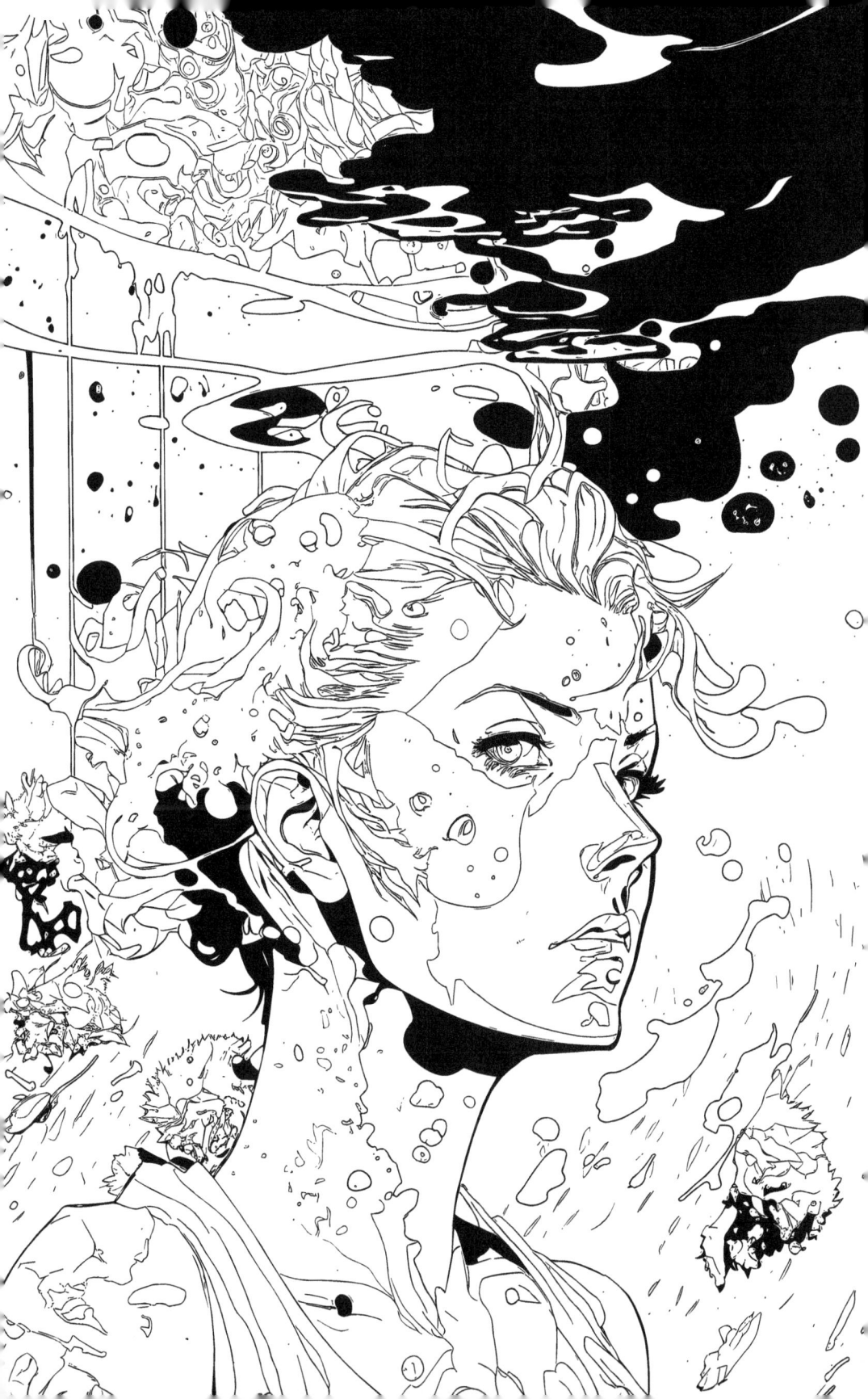

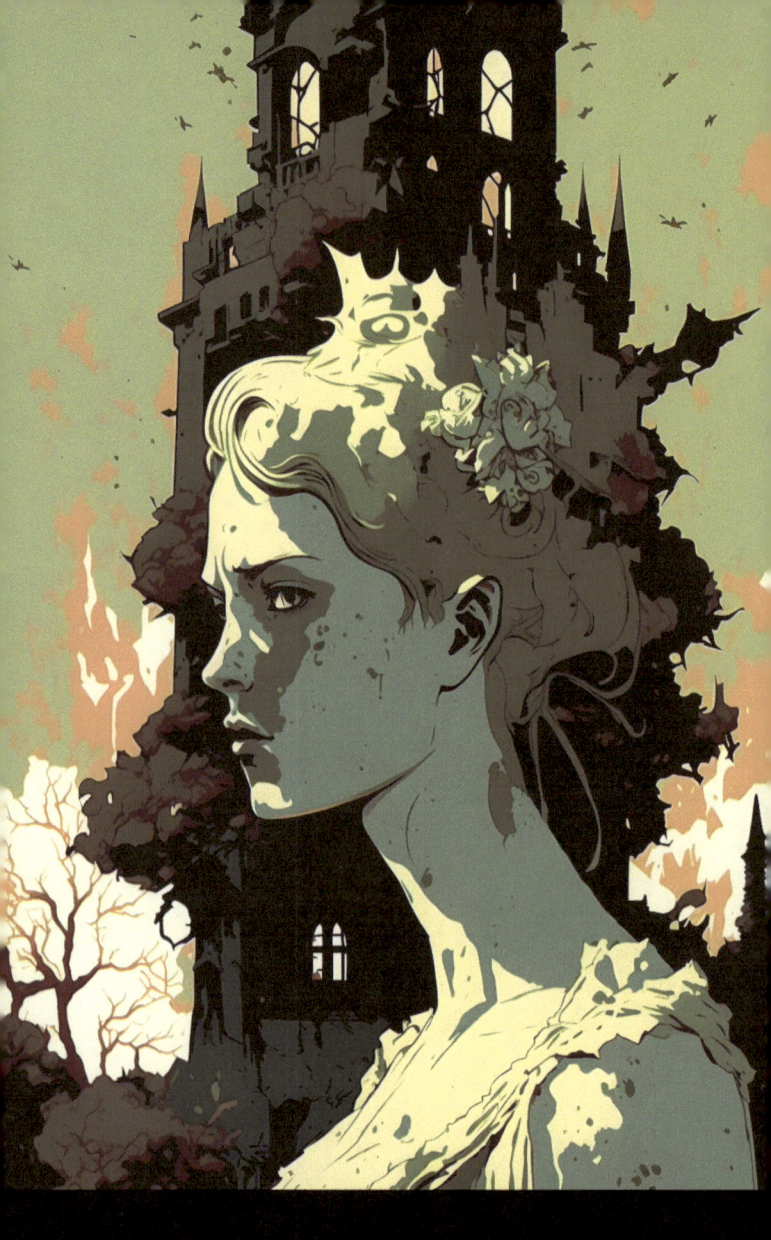

Dreams are the constellation of the spirit, illuminating the way to a deeper understanding of the self.

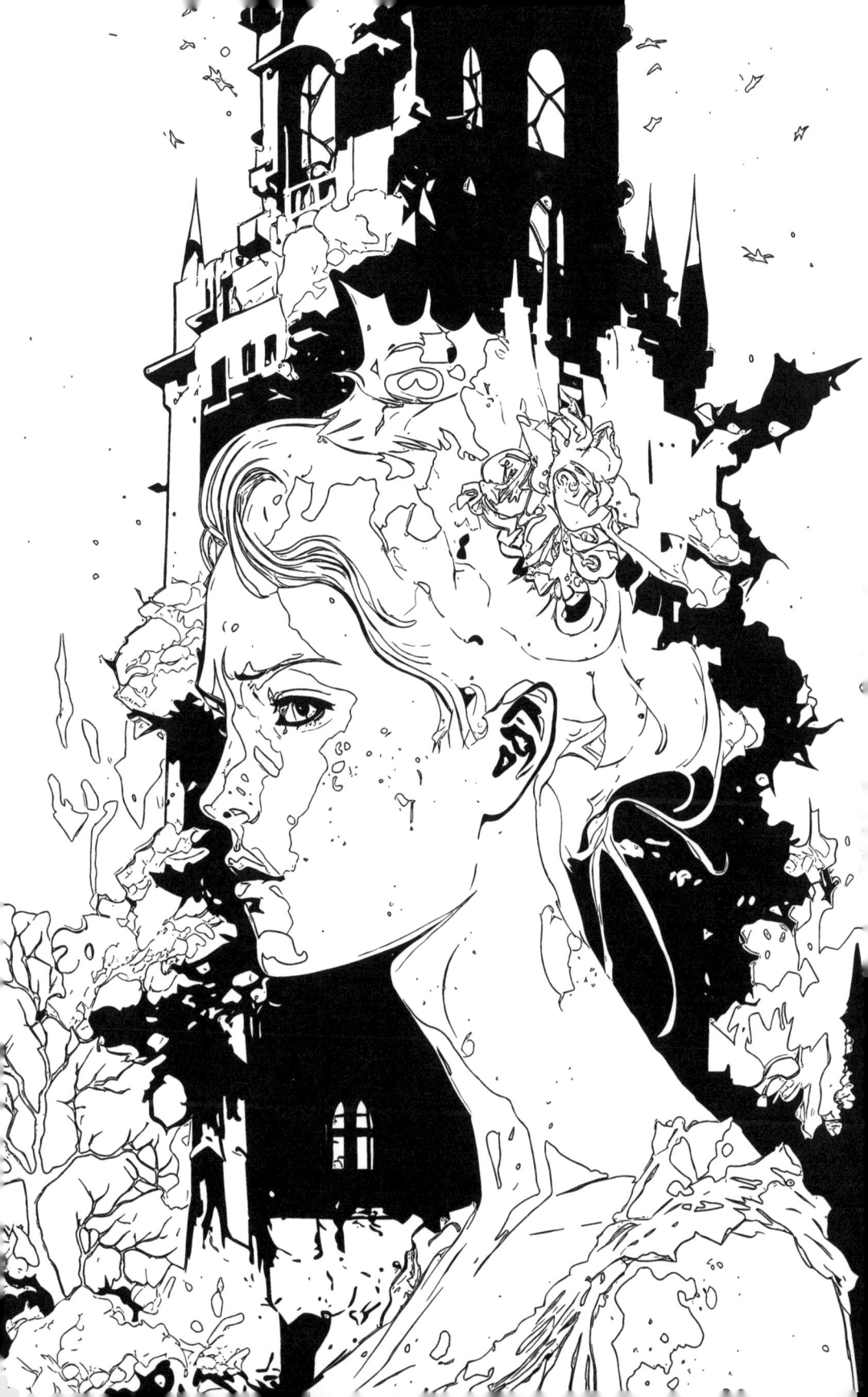

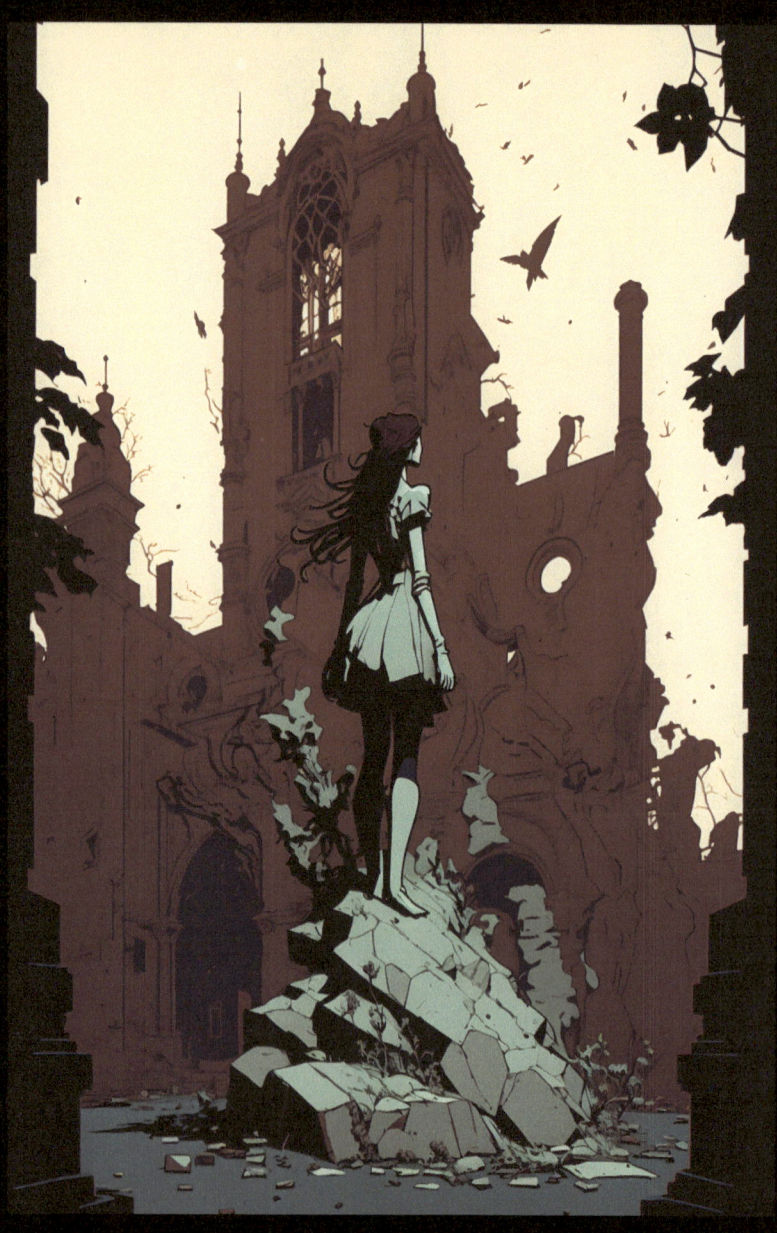

In the garden of the mind, dreams are the blossoms that awaken in the moonlight.

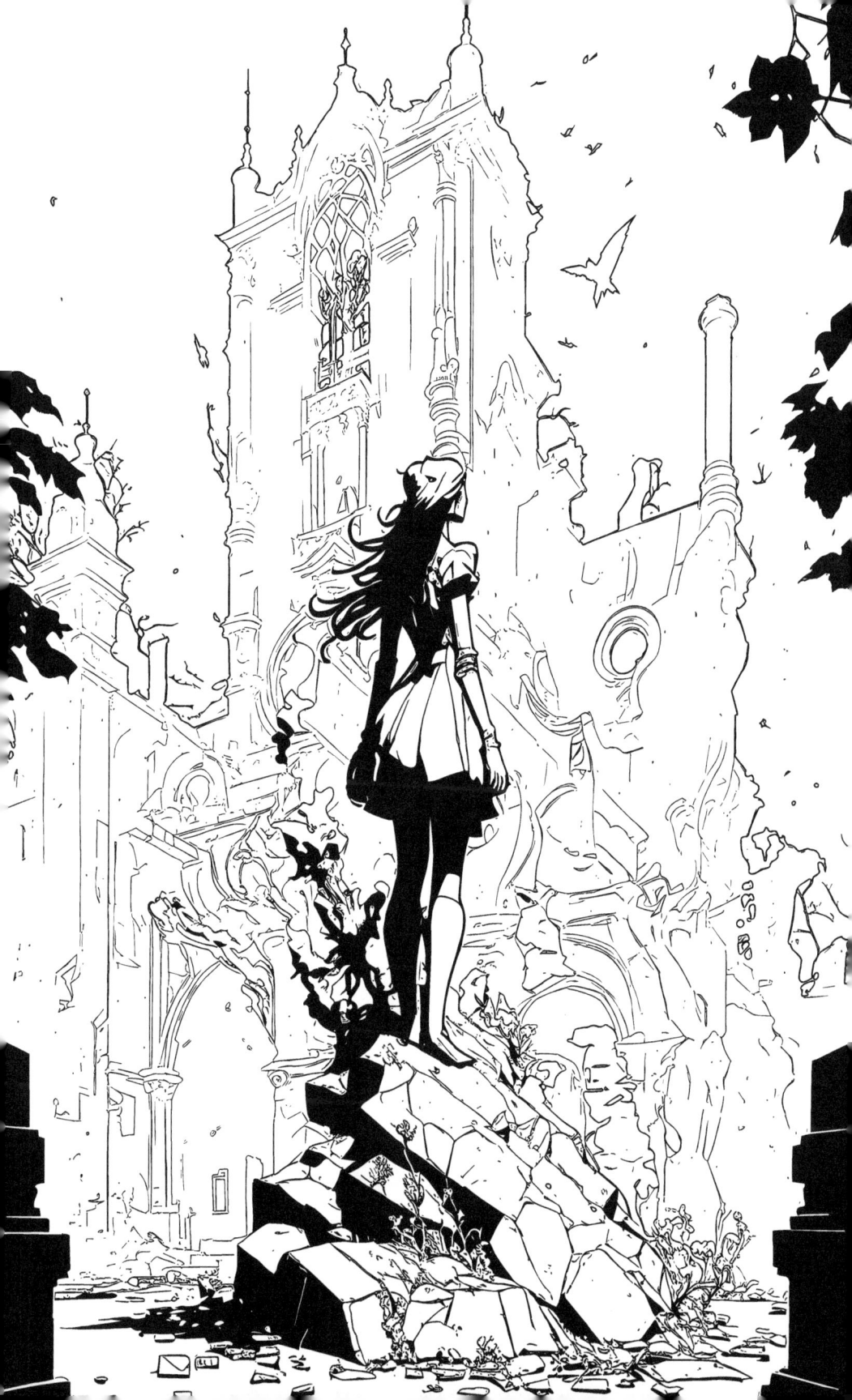

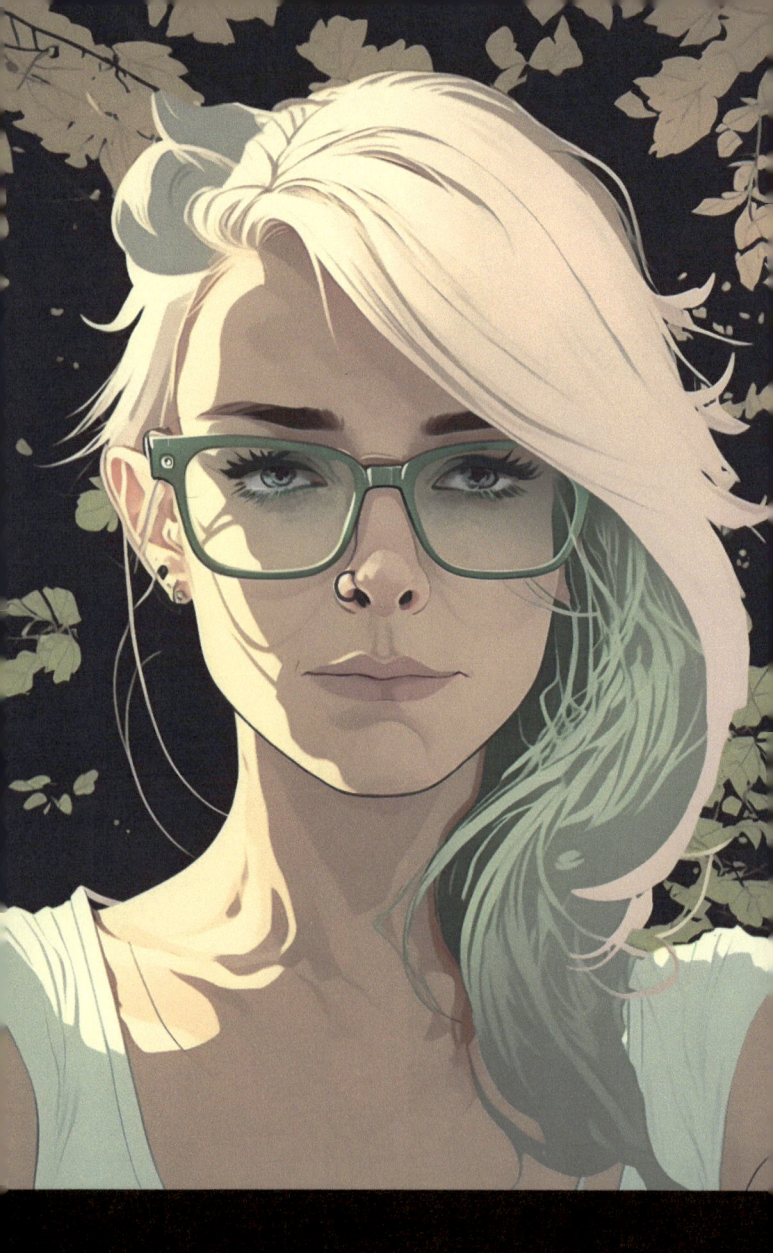

Dreams are the windows to the self, where hidden thoughts and feelings are illuminated.

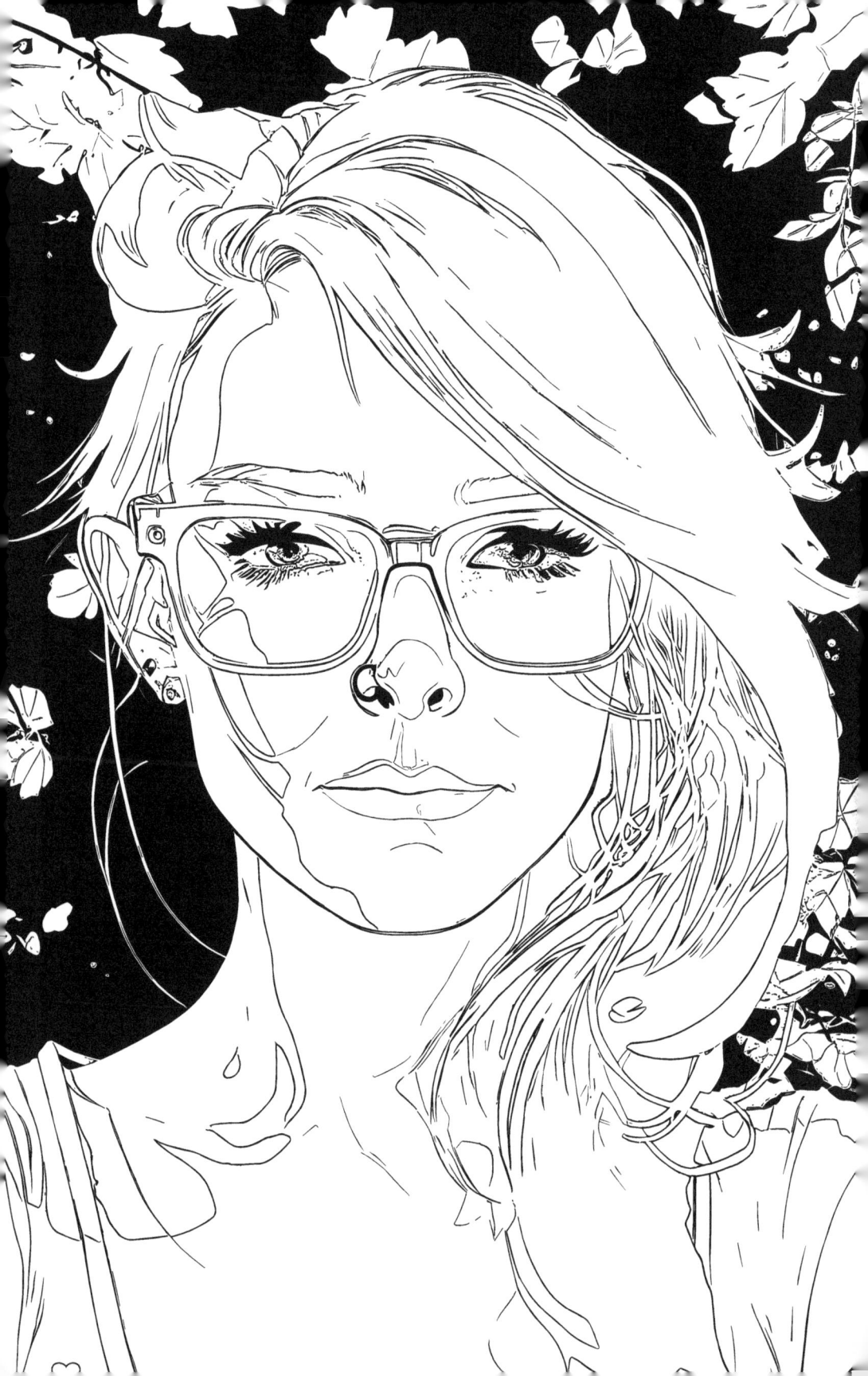

CHROMATIC DREAMS

CHROMATIC DREAMS